Arbeiter bei Haarmann & Reimer, 1950er
Workers at Haarmann & Reimer, 1950s

Friseursalon Gerberding, um 1910
Gerberding hairdressing salon, around 1910

Arbeiter am Dampfkessel von Haarmann & Reimer, 1920er
Worker at the Haarmann & Reimer steam boiler, 1920s

150 years of fragrances & flavors

Industrial history
in Holzminden
1874 - 2024

Published by the Local History Society for the District and Town of Holzminden e.V.

With the financial support of
Symrise AG and
Horst-Otto Gerberding

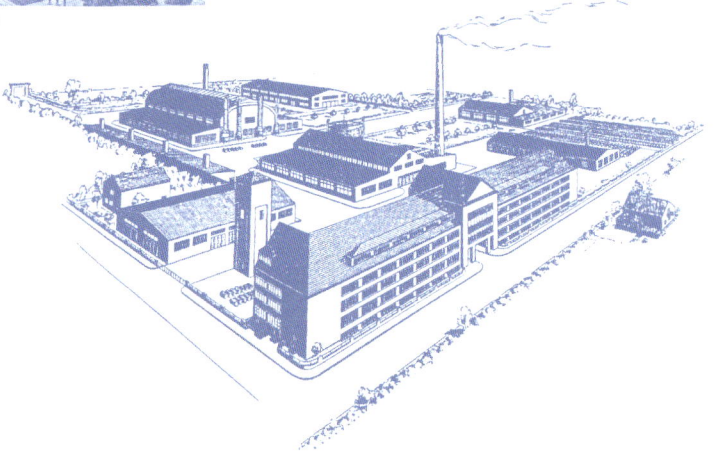

Bibliographic information of the German National Library. The German National Library lists this publication in the German National Bibliography; detailed bibliographic data are available on the internet at http://dnb.de.
ISBN 978-3-95954-165-87

All rights reserved.

Design: Verlag Jörg Mitzkat
Proofreading: Nina Schiefelbein

Verlag Jörg Mitzkat · Holzminden, 2024 · www.mitzkat.de

Jörg Mitzkat

150 *years of fragrances & flavors*

Industrial history in Holzminden 1874 - 2024

Verlag Jörg Mitzkat
Holzminden 2024

Contents

Introduction — 6

The Beginnings — 8
1874 - 1883
Excursus: The town of Holzminden and its citizens — 26

The Upswing — 28
1884 - 1918

New Beginnings and Another War — 50
1919 - 1945

The Dawn of the Post-War Period — 82
1945 - 1955
Excursus: Other Fragrance and Flavour Companies — 102

Worldwide Growth — 104
1956 - 2002

The Merger to Form Symrise — 134
2003 - today
Excursus: Regional Companies in Symrise's vicinity — 146

Appendix — 156

1874 - 1883

1884 - 1918

1919 - 1945

1945 - 1955

1956 - 2002

2003 - 2024

Introduction

On 2nd October, Dr. Wilhelm Haarmann Vanillin Factory was founded. The establishment of this company marks the birth of synthetic fragrance and flavour production and the beginning of industrial development in the Weser town of Holzminden.

This book aims to shed light on the development that has led to one of the world's most important companies involved in the development and production of fragrances and flavours being based in Holzminden today.

It is not a scientific work, even though the author was sometimes given this impression due to the numerous files which he came across in various contexts and whose significance had to be analysed. At best, however, it remains a spotlight on certain developments - especially in and after wartimes - that are worth analysing academically.

The book concentrates on the development in Holzminden which was initially dominated by the entrepreneur Wilhelm Haarmann and, then, from 1876, by his company which operated as Haarmann & Reimer.

In 1919, Carl Wilhelm Gerberding founded Dragoco, a second company in Holzminden within the fragrance and flavour industry. In terms of production technology, the first years were admittedly modest, but when stating the purpose of the company, Gerberding was already showing foresight and, having taken over an old iron foundry, was able to start industrial production in 1929.

Up until the beginning of the 21st century, both Holzminden-based companies existed in competition with each other and both were able to stand their ground and develop into respectable 'players' within the branch of fragrance and flavour producers. In 2002, the two companies merged to become Symrise, a company which, today, counts as one of the most important producers within this segment worldwide.

The townscape of Holzminden has been significantly influenced by these entrepreneurial activities. Starting with Wilhelm Haarmann's small shed on the

City map of Holzminden with the Symrise factory site

Holzminde stream in the former village of Altendorf, the production facilities, laboratories and administrative buildings have expanded into the town, and at the same time, the town has grown around these facilities and beyond. This did not always go smoothly but compromises were always found in the light of being mutually dependent.

If you consider a period of 150 years, global historical events and catastrophes move into focus; wars, violent regencies and economic crises have had a very serious impact on the Holzminden commercial enterprises. And maybe it is these current global crises which focus interest on how it has been possible for the people and, in this case, the companies which have been carried by these people, to survive the past crises.

For a company that relies on constant innovation, future viability is essential for survival. It is necessary to look at the successes and failures of earlier business decisions in order to assess how to continue to work and operate successfully in the future.

A glance at the last chapter, which covers little more than twenty years, shows that the future of the Holzminden site hung in the balance but it was saved thanks to the many people here in the area working together.

For the future, we can only hope that the international Group which has emerged from *Dr. Haarmann's Vanillin Factory in Altendorf* near Holzminden will not lose sight of those working for the good of the company in Holzminden.

View over Holzminden

Introduction

The Beginnings
1874 - 1883

The Beginnings

Holzminden c.1880: The photo above and the lithograph below show the town of Holzminden before the construction of the Weser bridge. In the foreground of the lithograph is the bridge over the harbour basin, behind which are stored slabs of Solling sandstone for shipment.
The Haarmann family was largely responsible for the trade in Solling sandstone, especially polished slabs for floors and roof coverings. Wilhelm Haarmann, the son of this family, was born in 1847 in the house on the right-hand side of the picture.

The systematic research of materials on a molecular and atomic level, the development of more exact analytic methods and, finally, the discovery of structure formulas of the chemical elements brought far reaching progress in chemical knowledge in the 19th century. In particular, the discoveries made by Friedrich Wöhler contributed to the establishment of organic synthetic chemistry as a new research field. The synthesis of natural materials from various base materials, which were often readily available, was the cornerstone for the development of the chemical industry. Germany was a leading light in this field up until the First World War.

Foundation of the First Chemical Company

The scientific discoveries were first used for the industrial production of dyes: the companies Bayer and Hoechst were founded in 1863 as dyestuff factories; Badische Anilin- und Sodafabrik (BASF) (Baden Aniline and Soda Factory) was established in 1865; and in 1867, AGFA (Aktien-Gesellschaft für Anilin-Fabrikation) (public limited company for Aniline Production) was founded to produce dyestuffs and primary products on the basis of aniline, which serves as the base material for the synthesis of dyes and man-made fibres.

History of Fragrances and Aromas

The history of the development and use of fragrance and aroma materials is tightly interwoven with the cultural history of mankind. Fragrances can trigger an immediate feeling and memory. The term perfume is derived from the Latin term 'per fumum', which means 'with the help of smoke'. Way back in history, mankind ascertained that various smells, sometimes pleasantly smelling perfumes, evolved by burning wood and herbs. Vessels in which fragrant herbs and salves were stored have been traced back to 5000 BC. Further finds indicate that the technology of distillation was being developed as early as 3000 BC. Distillation was used to

Friedrich Wöhler – pioneer of organic chemistry

Friedrich Wöhler (* 31 July 1800 in Eschersheim; † 23 September 1882 in Göttingen) is considered a pioneer of organic chemistry. His syntheses of oxalic acid by hydrolysis of prussic acid (1824) and of urea from ammonium cyanate (1828) established biochemistry, as for the first time substances that had previously only been known from living organisms could be artificially produced from inanimate matter. Initially, these syntheses received little public attention. Wöhler was a close friend of Justus von Liebig. Together with Liebig, he established the radical theory around 1830. This enabled the great variety of organic chemical compounds to be systematically explained for the first time. With their plant chemical research, Wöhler's students laid a further foundation for the establishment of biochemistry as a separate branch of science.

Antique fragrance vessels, Greece

1874 – 1883

Birthplace of Wilhelm Haarmann on the banks of the Weser in Holzminden

produce essential oils from herbs and the volatile fragrant substances were separated from their solid carrier materials and could be conserved in tightly sealed jars for a long time. Purely on the technical side, the production of fragrant materials did not change in principle until the first synthetisation in the 19th century. However, the manufacturing processes and the numerous fragrant notes had been continuously refined.

While the significance of fragrant materials was initially connected to religion, fine perfumes were probably already luxury goods and status symbols in ancient Egypt. The perfumes of modern times have their origins in France. The development of perfumes was originally linked to the production of fine leather materials. In the late 16th century, fine leather gloves came into fashion but the penetrating smell of the tanned leather had to be disguised by fine perfumes. For this reason, the leather and perfume industries joined forces in Grasse. As the fine fragrance business was more profitable in the long term, the tanners eventually became fragrance manufacturers. To this day, the town in the south of France is considered the global centre of fragrances.

In Germany, it was Leipzig which started to become a centre for the manufacture of essential oils and essences from the beginning of the 19th century. The most important protagonist of this early fragrance industry was the company Schimmel & Co. This company will be mentioned in this book several times.

Grave of the Haarmann family in the Allersheimer Strasse cemetery in Holzminden. However, Wilhelm Haarmann was buried in Höxter, where he had later lived.

The Beginnings

The Haarmann Family in Holzminden

The history of Holzminden on the river Weser is tightly interwoven with the Haarmann family in the 18th and 19th centuries. Friedrich Ludwig Haarmann founded the School of Architecture in Holzminden in 1864 and it was the first of its type in Germany. Today, the school is an integral part of HAWK (University of Applied Sciences and Arts) Göttingen / Hildesheim / Holzminden. Further members of the family were involved in the quarrying, processing and sale of Solling sandstone. Heinrich Wilhelm Haarmann, father of Wilhelm Haarmann (born in 1847), was one of them. It is possible that, as early as the middle of the 1860s, father Heinrich Wilhelm had already recognised that chemistry would play a significant role in the development of the economy. An entry in the family chronicles by his son Wilhelm Haarmann is an indication of this.

He wrote about his father: "*Later, when he was a self-employed merchant and manufacturer he often dealt with problems of mechanics, chemistry etc.*" After a happy childhood in tranquil Holzminden, Wilhelm Haarmann initially went to study chemistry at the Bergakademie (Mountain Academy) in Clausthal, before transferring to the University of Göttingen a year later, as he had spent "*an enjoyable year with friends*" in Clausthal, but "*with few scientific achievements*". *This was to change in Göttingen where he came into contact with Friedrich Wöhler who held the Chair of Pharmacy and Chemistry there. Wilhelm Haarmann writes in the family chronicles:* "*It was thanks to the latter that I was able to work with the rarest of metals, with platinum. 3 semesters later, I was drawn to Hofmann in Berlin who was the foremost authority in the field of organic chemistry.*"

1870s – Chemical Institute of Berlin

Chemist August Wilhelm Hofmann, as of 1888 von Hofmann, was a pioneer for the research of aniline dyes in England and Germany. He developed a multitude of important methods of transformation in organic chemistry. Hofmann founded the German Chemical Society of Berlin in 1867. As of May 1865, he held lectures

August Wilhelm von Hofmann
The chemist August Wilhelm Hofmann, from 1888 von Hofmann (* 8. April 1818 in Giessen; † 5. Mai 1892 in Berlin), was a pioneer in the research of aniline dyes. He developed a large number of important synthesis methods in organic chemistry. Hofmann was married four times and had eleven children; three of his wives died early. He married his fourth wife, Bertha Tiemann (1854-1922), in 1873. She outlived him by 30 years. Bertha was the sister of his assistant Ferdinand Tiemann. Tiemann, a friend of Wilhelm Haarmann and silent partner of the Holzminden company, was also for many years the editor of the reports of the German Chemical Society, which were published by Hofmann. The Chemical Institute on Georgenstrasse, founded by August Wilhelm von Hofmann, was one of the most important chemical research and training centres in Europe during the 30 years of its existence. Around 300 doctoral theses were supervised there. Almost 900 scientific publications "from the Berlin University laboratory", 150 of them by Hofmann himself, testify to a high level of scientific productivity.

The Chemical Institute on Georgenstrasse, Berlin, c.1870

1874 – 1883

Group picture at the 1st Chemical Institute on Georgenstrasse, Berlin. Among others, the future H&R chemists Dr. Schmidt and Dr. Lemme are pictured here, c.1880

Synthesis (Chemistry)
In chemistry, synthesis (from the Greek - 'composition') refers to the process by which a compound is produced from elements or a complicated, composite new substance is created from simple compounds. (Synthetic) synthesis is the exemplary creation of a compound on a laboratory scale, but also the creation of an element in its pure form. A synthesis is, therefore, more than the (physical) mixing of two or more substances. In contrast to a mixture, the starting materials cannot be recovered from a newly synthesised compound by purely physical processes.

in the 1st Chemical Institute of Berlin both in inorganic and organic chemistry. Ferdinand Tiemann became von Hoffmann's assistant in 1869.

Wilhelm Haarmann received important impulses for his research in von Hoffmann's laboratory, where he met Ferdinand Tiemann. Haarmann wrote about this in his family chronicles, which he seemingly completed years later from memory: "*In May 69, I found my Göttingen and Holzminden friends there again and through them made the acquaintance of Ferd. Tiemann, with whom I worked side by side in the laboratory. This gradually developed into an intimate friendship, which was only torn apart by Tiemann's death in November 1899.*"

1870/71 – Franco-Prussian War

In 1870/71 Haarmann and Tiemann left to fight in the Franco-Prussian War. They were assigned to different regiments and did not see each other again until after the war in the autumn of 1871. Wilhelm Haarmann's regiment remained in France until the late summer.

The Beginnings

Wilhelm Haarmann (right)
Ferdinand Tiemann (left)

The research of a Holzminden apothecary

Tiemann gave Haarmann an important piece of advice regarding vanillin. He was familiar with the incomplete research results of the Holzminden apothecary Wilhelm Kubel who had researched the cambial sap of conifers with Theodor Hartig, the Brunswick forest scientist. Hartig was able to convince Kubel to hand over a small amount of 8 grammes to Haarmann when he visited Holzminden. The inaugural dissertation had been approved by the University of Göttingen and was titled *About Some Derivatives of the Glucosides Coniferin and Salicin*. Wilhelm Haarmann used the laboratory of August Wilhelm von Hoffmann in Berlin to carry out his research. In April 1872 Wilhelm Haarmann passed with summa cum laude.

The vanilla aroma was, in fact, only a by-product of the dissertation but Tiemann and Haarmann followed this avenue with undiminished energy. However, they needed a much larger quantity of coniferin. "*Through my father's kindness, I came into possession of fir trees, I scraped and boiled and, in July, I had 500 grammes of coniferin for further examination in Berlin, with Tiemann, who was living as an assistant in the laboratory and who took me in and supported me.*"

Even before Tiemann and Haarmann could complete their research, both scientists travelled as part of a field trip "*to England's factories!*" The next entry in Haarmann's family chronicles sounds laconic but was extremely important for the future paths of these two chemists: "*In Febr. 1873 the result, vanillin was completed, patents were taken out.*"

The significance of the vanilla flavouring and, thus, the potential that would lie in the artificial reproduction of the vanilla flavour clearly motivated Wilhelm Haarmann to push ahead with the project. The production of artificial fertilisers and synthetic dyes were role models for the potential business success.

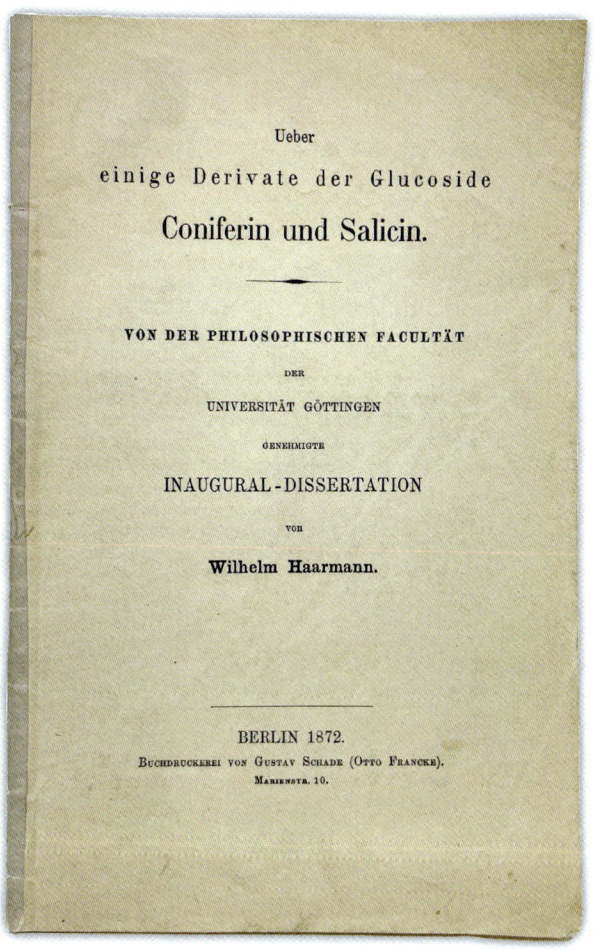

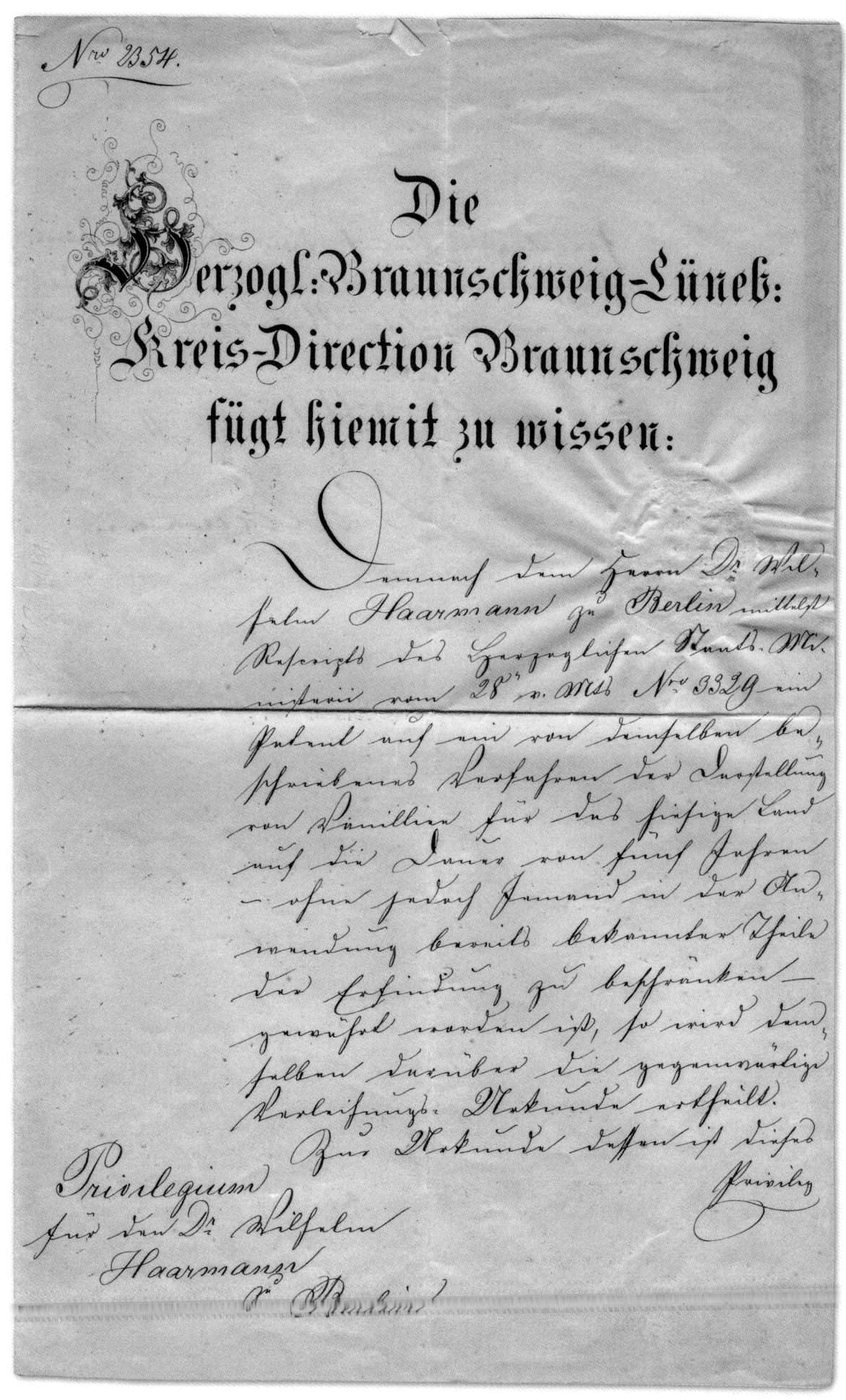

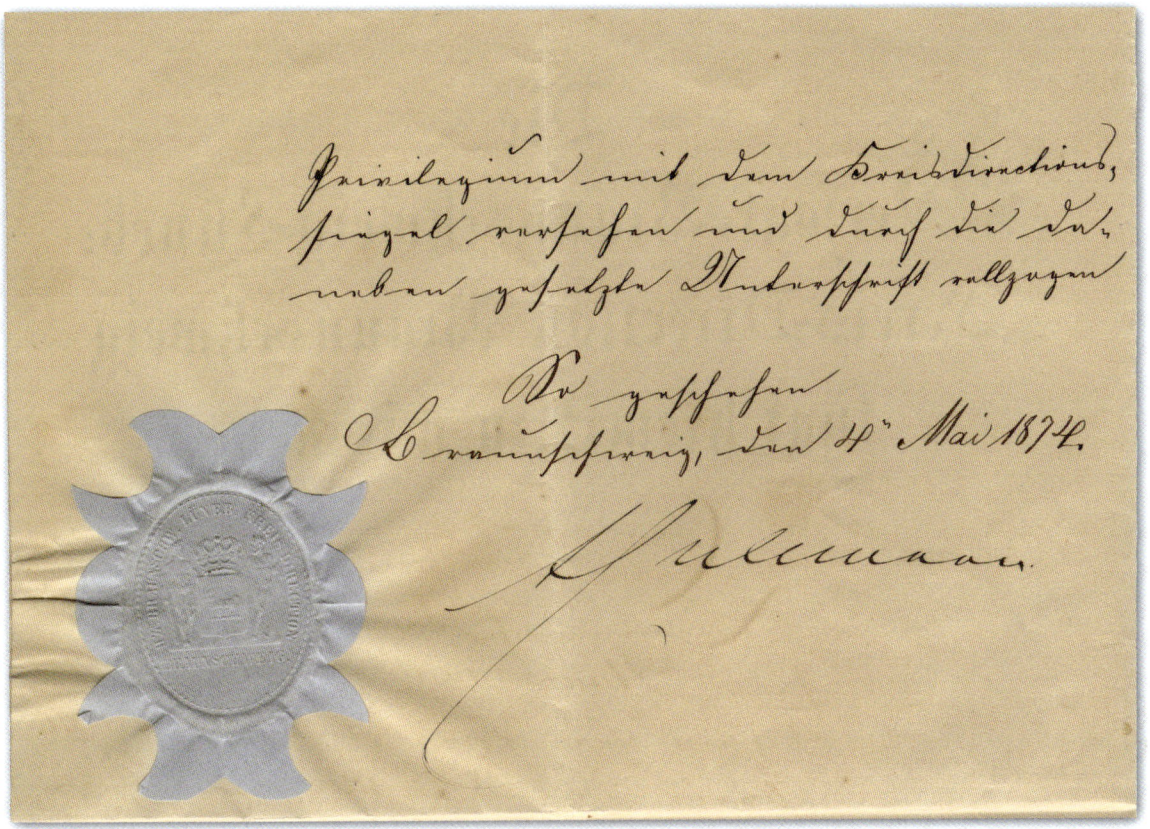

In March, he travelled to Oberhof in Thuringia to collect further material. However, the amount of four kilos was not sufficient. Seeing as cambial sap can only be extracted in spring, Haarmann devoted himself to other interests in the second half of the year. It is quite obvious that he had his sights firmly set on industrial production. The family chronicles state: *"In autumn and winter learned glass production in Silberborn."*

Photo top and left: licence granted by the Ducal Brunswick-Lüneburg District Administration to Dr. Wilhelm Haarmann, Berlin, for the manufacture of vanillin, May 1874

1874 – Foundation of Dr. Wilhelm Haarmann Vanillin Factory
In 1874, Wilhelm Haarmann finally achieved his goal: *"In spring, working with enthusiasm in Oberhof but after visiting Silesia and Bohemia, failure. Continuation in the Black Forest in Baden, Gernsbach near Rastadt. Success. Material 20 kg in sight. Father's barite shed is converted into a laboratory and small factory. Company Dr.W.H."* This is the beginning of an industrial history of fragrances and flavours that has lasted for 150 years.

It was in the same year that international patents were registered for the production of vanillin, amongst others in England and Canada. Ferdinand Tiemann became a sleeping partner of the company.

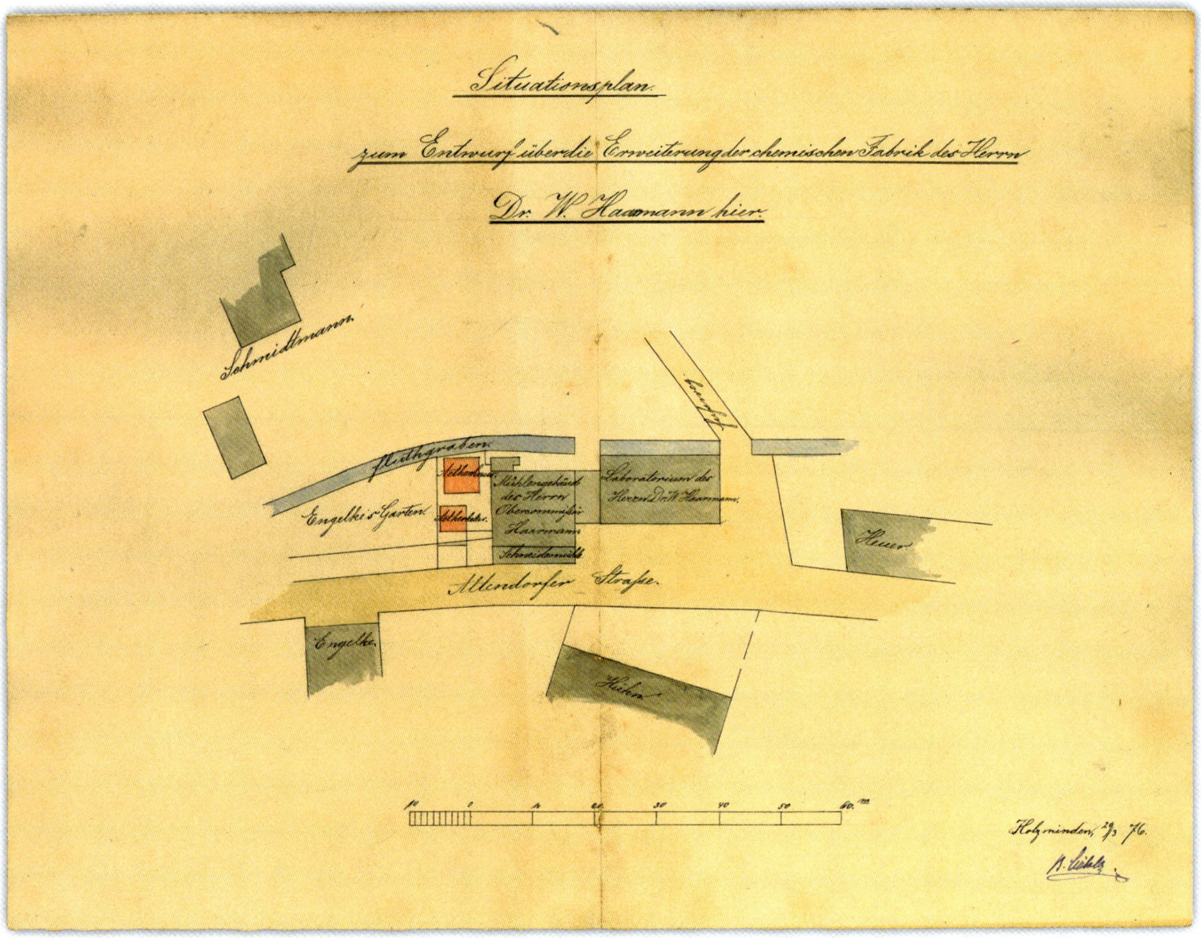

As early as 1876, Wilhelm Haarmann expanded the 'factory' he had set up in his father's shed.

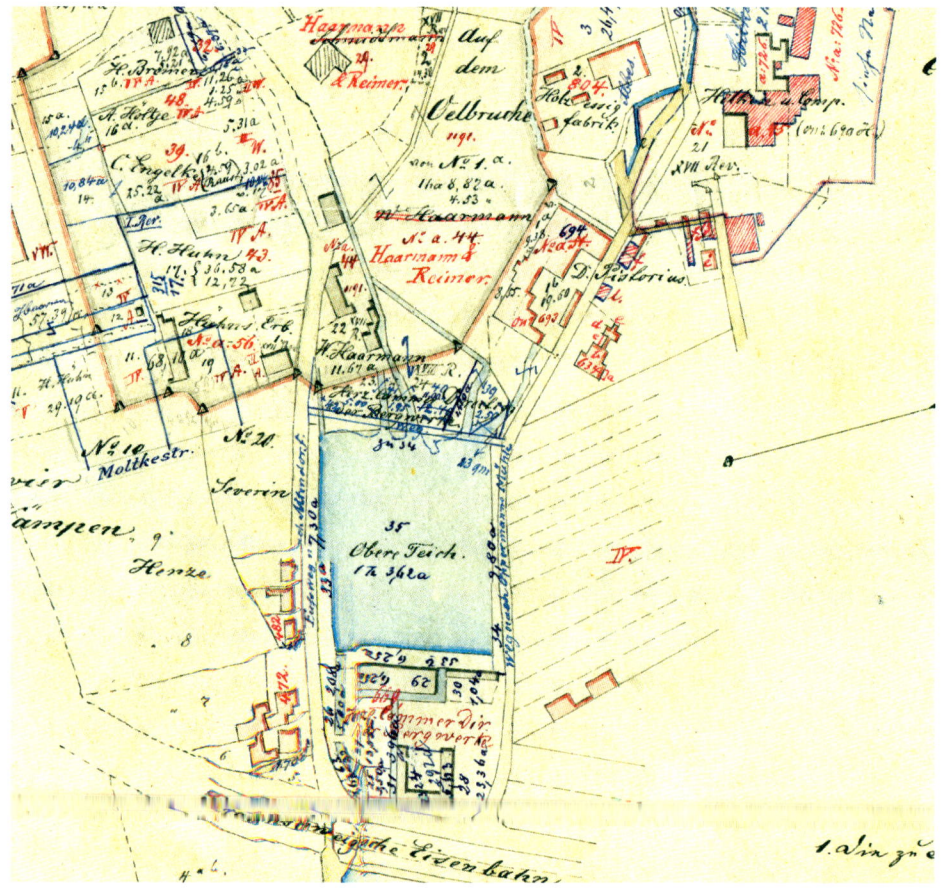

This map of the district boundaries in the fields between Holzminden and Altendorf dates from 1886. The newly acquired Haarmann & Reimer land is marked in red. However, the writing "W. Haarmann" in grey, along with the buildings marked next to it and above it directly above the upper pond, provides a good indication of Wilhelm Haarmann's first production plant.

The Beginnings

Vanilla and vanillin

Vanilla is not considered a classic fragrance. The plant originates from Mexico. The typical vanilla flavour is only obtained after the time-consuming and labour-intensive curing process and subsequent fermentation of the vanilla fruit capsules. The scent and flavour of vanilla only came to Europe after the conquest of America whereby it had already been known in Central America for a long time. The Totonaks, who were later dominated by the Aztec ruler Itzcoatl, were probably the first and only people to produce vanilla for a long time. Even then, it was enjoyed in combination with cocoa, the sharp taste of which was rounded off by the sweet vanilla flavour. It is likely that Hernán Cortés was the first European to taste vanilla, at the court of Montezuma II. Vanilla was said to have aphrodisiac properties and the fact that Spain guarded its monopoly on the export and trade of vanilla until Mexico gained its independence in 1821 certainly contributed to the mystique surrounding vanilla. Its consumption was reserved for the rich and powerful. It was only at the beginning of the 19th century that cuttings of vanilla plants first arrived in European botanical gardens. However, the best conditions for this climbing plant to thrive are only found in tropical rainforests around the equator. The so-called Bourbon vanilla was first cultivated by the French on the Île de Bourbon, now known as La Réunion. However, there were some initial problems here as well. It is only in Central America that vanilla can be pollinated naturally by hummingbirds and certain insects. Although vanilla can sometimes find good growing conditions on the islands in the Indian Ocean, it has to be pollinated by hand. Today, a large proportion of natural vanilla production comes from Madagascar and Indonesia, where the flowers, which only open for a short time, must also be pollinated by hand.

Due to the natural unmanageability of vanilla plants, vanilla has remained a valuable and rare flavouring agent to this day. This was all the more true during the times of Wilhelm Haarmann, who was born in Holzminden in the mid-19th century: Not only was vanilla highly sought after, it was also very expensive. It was for this reason that the plant soon became the focus of chemical research: In 1858, Frenchman Nicolas-Théodore Gobley succeeded in isolating vanillin as the main flavouring agent in vanilla extract and in establishing an initial molecular formula. Although this was still inaccurate, it pointed other researchers in the right direction until Wilhelm Haarmann and Ferdinand Tiemann were finally able to analyse the substance chemically without doubt in 1873.

Historical representation of the vanilla harvest in Mexico on Liebig trading cards, c.1900.

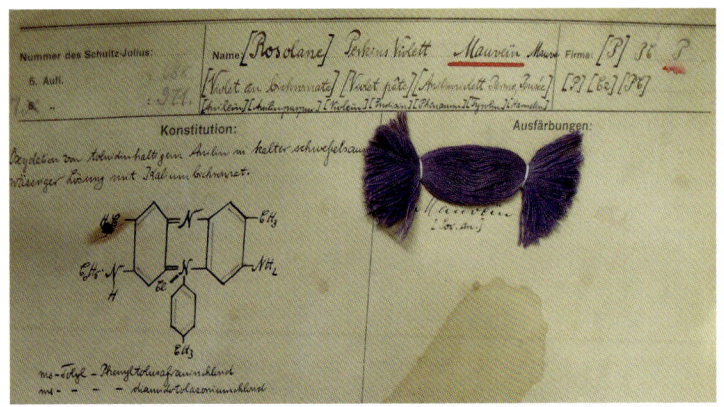

Mauveine was the first synthetic dye. It was discovered by accident by the Englishman William Henry Perkin in 1856 while he was trying to synthesize quinine. The picture shows a sample in the historical dye collection of the TU Dresden.

Scientific findings are applied – the chemical industry is born

With the founding of the company, Haarmann and Tiemann followed several role models who also dared to risk moving from successful chemical research to the production of new products. The results of the chemical research were first put into practice in the manufacture of dyes and fertilisers.

Bayer was founded in 1863 and began with the manufacture of dyes; Hoechst and Kalle were also established in the same year; BASF was founded in 1865; Aktiengesellschaft für Anilinfabrikation (AGFA – Joint Stock Company for Aniline Production) began in 1867 and in 1870 Casella Dye Company was founded.

Georges de Laire

1875 – First international relations

The company established international ties in the first year of its existence. Tiemann travelled to Paris to set up a partnership with Georges de Laire, who he knew from the Hofmann laboratory in Berlin. If a patent was applied for a process in France, then, due to legal requirements, this process had also to be used in France. As part of its partnership with Tiemann and Haarmann, De Laire & Co. switched its production to vanillin.

Just a few years after the end of the Franco-German war, this was quite a remarkable co-operation. The two companies acquired shares in each other.

Karl Reimer

1876 – Karl Reimer joined the company – Haarmann & Reimer

Karl Reimer succeeded in producing vanillin from guaiacol using the Tiemann-Reimer synthesis. This method made vanillin production considerably cheaper. Haarmann offered Reimer the opportunity to join the company as a partner. The new company name was Haarmann & Reimer Vanillinfabrik in Holzminden an der Weser (Haarmann & Reimer Vanillin Factory in Holzminden on the Weser). In this year, Wilhelm Haarmann and Ferdinand Tiemann received the Cothenius Medal from the renowned Leopoldina Academy for their research work.

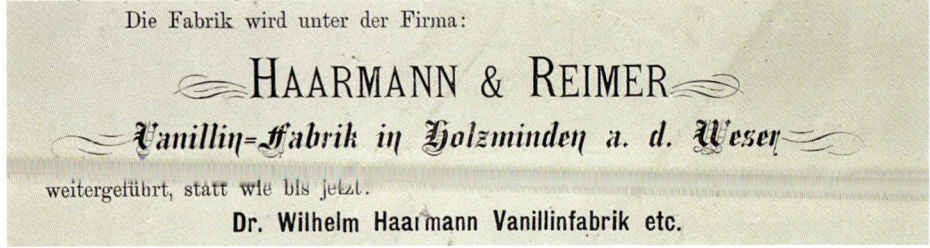

The Beginnings

1876 – Presentation at the World Exhibition in Philadelphia

A report on the 1876 World Exhibition in Philadelphia describes some of the small glass tubes exhibited there as containing *"one of the most extraordinary preparations of the German chemical department, namely the aromatic substance of the vanilla pod, produced by Dr. Wilhelm Haarmann in Holzminden on the Weser"*. Being present at the World Exhibition shows that the founders of Haarmann & Reimer were convinced of their product, even though commercial success had yet to materialise.

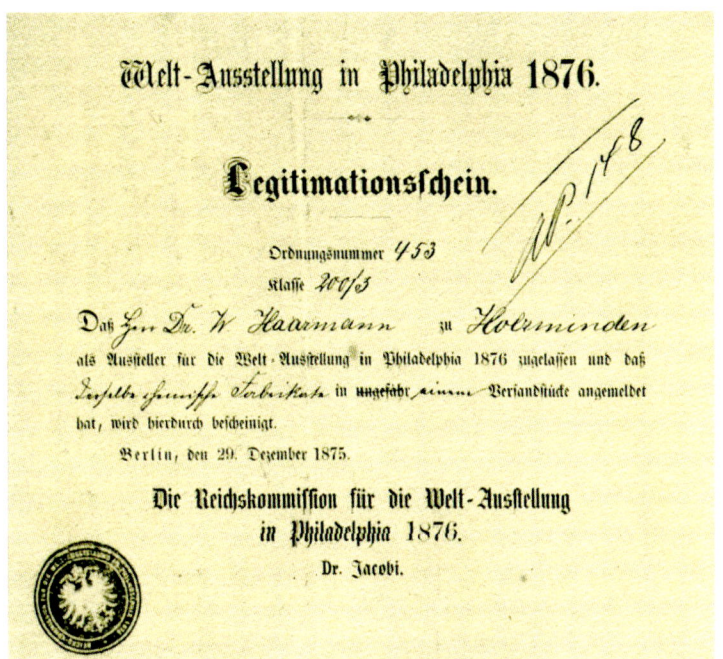

Certificate of eligibility for the 1876 World Exhibition

1877 – First patent in the German Empire

The Imperial Patent Office was established which meant that patents could now be applied for throughout the German Empire. The granting of the first German imperial patent marked the beginning of one of Haarmann & Reimer's entrepreneurially vital, but, as it turns out, very arduous tasks. In contrast to the USA, German patent law only protected the manufacturing process and not the new substance. Substance protection was only introduced in German patent law in 1968. Until then, the patent holder had to prove that the competitor was using the same manufacturing process.

1878 – New products for the first time

From 1878, Haarmann & Reimer was also able to offer other products. Coumarin, in particular, which was produced in Germany and France for perfumery and snuff production, proved to be commercially promising.

Karl Reimer left the company as early as 1881 due to ill health. However, it was thanks to his research that the use of eugenol, which was obtained from clove oil, led to a significantly better yield of vanillin. By 1881, the company was actually making a profit.

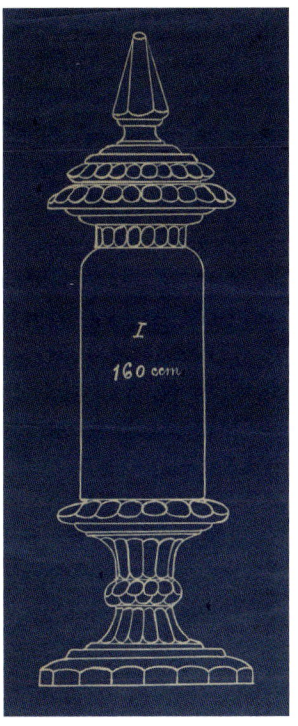

Container for presenting vanillin at the 1871 World Exhibition

1874 – 1883

On 22 January 1876, Dr Wilh. Haarmann himself signed for the delivery of a "crate of chemicals" that had been sent by express freight via the German railway to Holzminden.

An uphill climb to the first commercial success

It was a difficult climb for the young company until then. Wilhelm Haarmann's belief in vanillin must have been unshakeable as the entries in his family chronicles bear witness to many setbacks and great worries. As early as 1874, he noted about the establishment of the company: "*Apothecary Koken as an assistant, atrocious.*" Although he was able to announce the first sale of vanillin at 9 marks a gramme in 1875, "*vanilla dealer Gröner in Berlin [...] later proves to be a scoundrel.*" In those early days, it is quite obvious that Wilhelm Haarmann was also involved with the production. He wrote: "*Dismissed Koken in autumn. Accepted clerk Grain. [...] Worked hard through the winter.*"

On 11th May 1876, Wilhelm Haarmann married Luise Stieren. However, the bridegroom even worked for the factory while on his honeymoon: "*Honeymoon to Gernsbach where I also check things out on the side.*" It was near Gernsbach in the Black Forest where the valuable raw material coniferin was extracted.

However, a year later it was still not looking any better: "*1877 coniferin sparse, must work with eugenol. Hard work. Failures, serious worries.*"

Poor results: Haarmann & Reimer's annual report from 1877

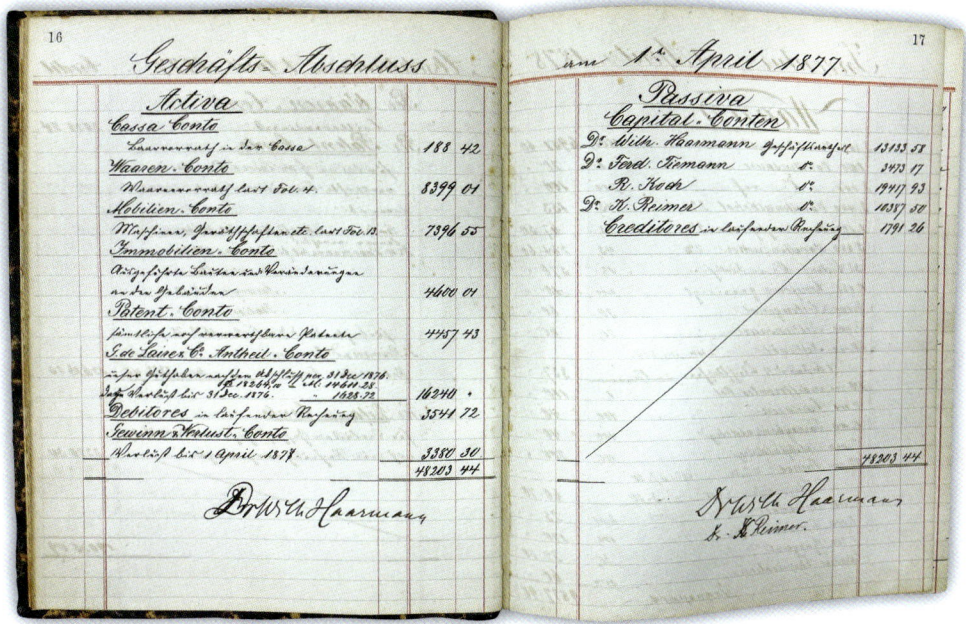

In 1878, the situation in Haarmann's review also hardly changed: "*1878: Further failures in production despite the most arduous work. Serious worries. Grote is taken as office clerk.*"

One year later and a ray of hope: "*1879 first better success with eugenol. Reimer's idea. In this and the following years, many trips, Berlin, conference with Tiemann and twice a year to Paris.*"

Haarmann wrote about the year 1880: "*Production and sales improve.*" 1881 then: "*Production and sales increase, but always hard work. [...] 29th July – 9th Aug. Gustav H. [W. Haarmann's cousin] and I to Norway. Production is so successful that I was able to give 4000 M. to Uncle Fritz H. who was in debt.*"

1883 – Karl Reimer dies

W. W. Hoffmann, President of the Germany Chemical Society, composed an extensive obituary. In recognition of Karl Reimer's merits, his name remained part of the company name. The year was not only overshadowed by his death, it also marked the beginning of nerve-wracking years of patent disputes: "*The beginning of a major patent dispute because of eugenol. Most troublesome worries.*"

An advertisement for Haarmann & Reimer's vanillin, packaged in sachets with sugar, appeared in the Cologne newspaper on 3 May 1878 between advertisements for "fresh sole" and

In 1878, the newly established Imperial Patent Office granted the first patent in the empire for Haarmann's "process for artificially producing vanillin".

The Beginnings

The greatest effort ...

In Wilhelm Haarmann's obituary in the journal Riechstoff-Industrie (Aroma Industry), the chemist Dr. Albert Ellmer from Geneva vividly described the initial difficulties involved in obtaining coniferin for vanillin production:

Portrait of Wilhelm Haarmann as a successful businessman in the 1920s

"The greatest effort and the longest time were required in the first stage of manufacture to collect the coniferin required as a starting material. Only in spring does the cambial sap form between the trunk and bark and is then absorbed by the young shoots of spruce and fir trees as they sprout. However, the trees are felled in winter while the vegetation is dormant, i.e. at a time when no cambial sap and, therefore, no coniferin can be extracted. Only in some areas of the Thuringian and Black Forest, which are high and impassable in winter, are the trees felled and stripped in spring. This is where the interests of the young factory owner met those of the forestry industry. In the spring, under the leadership of a guide, columns of 20-30 women were sent to these remote districts where the sap was won. The bark was removed from the freshly felled trees and the layer containing the cambial sap was scraped off using broken glass, and the sap itself was extracted from this by soaking it up with sponges. Pots were taken along in which to sterilise the sap on the spot, by boiling it with water in order to remove the coniferin from the influence of destructive fermentation. The material, thus painstakingly obtained, was transported to Holzminden and processed there. On the one hand, the arduous process of extracting the raw material inevitably stood in the way of large-scale production. In the first year, 30 kg and in the second 80 kg were produced. On the other hand, the high price - vanillin originally cost 6,000 marks - prevented its extensive use in perfumery and chocolate production."

Handcarts on Halbmondstrasse in

Holzminden in the 19th century

View of Holzminden with the recently opened Weser bridge, c.1890

In order to appreciate the significance of the foundation of Wilhelm Haarmann's company in one of the most progressive economic sectors, it is helpful to take a brief look at life in the Weser town of Holzminden at the time: The founding of the vanillin factory in Altendorf near Holzminden came at a time when horse-drawn carts and handcarts characterised the townscape and the majority of Holzminden's population of around 6,000 people were employed in agriculture or farmed as a sideline. At the end of the 18th century, thanks to the economic development measures of Duke Carl I of Brunswick, a number of manufactories e.g. the glassworks in Grünenplan and the Fürstenberg porcelain factory were established in the Brunswick Weser district, now the district of Holzminden. However, compared to the number of people working in agriculture, the proportion of factory workers was still negligible. Thus, Wilhelm Haarmann initially had to recruit completely unskilled labourers for his up-and-coming vanilla factory. There were also no houses available to rent. Therefore, the factory also had to provide housing for the newly recruited labourers from the surrounding area.

Holzminden was connected to the railway network in 1865 via the Altenbeken-Kreiensen line. The connection between the Brunswick Southern Railway and the Royal Westphalian Railway Company created an important long-distance connection to the Rhineland-Westphalian industrial area and, from 1868, to Berlin via Magdeburg. This railway connection was probably an important prerequisite for Haarmann's decision to establish his vanillin factory in Altendorf near Holzminden. The site at Oberer Teich was located to the north-east, and only a short distance from the railway station. Around 1870, Fabrikstrasse (later Rumohrtalstrasse) was also constructed there, along which further industrial and commercial enterprises settled. Bernhard Liebold's cement and concrete goods factory was founded in 1881 on the Wilhelmshütte site to the south of the railway station.

At the same time as Haarmann's vanilla factory was founded, the Holzminden volunteer fire brigade was established. The first municipal hospital was built in 1879 and the town received a centralised water supply in 1888.

In the 1880s and 1890s, further industrial and commercial enterprises were established, but Holzminden's industrial capacities remained quite modest. It was not until around 1900 that Holzminden's population reached the 10,000 mark. With the founding of the glassworks, Weser-Sperrholzwerke (plywood works) and Otto Sasse GmbH, factories were established in the 20th century in which several hundred people quickly found work.

The population of Holzminden doubled after the end of the Second World War due to the arrival of refugees and displaced persons. The establishment of Stiebel Eltron and the boom in the chemical industry created many new jobs and Holzminden finally changed from a farming town to an industrial town.

Holzminden station, c.1890

Industrialisation

The industrial revolution took place much later in Germany than in England, where Wilhelm Haarmann had visited factories in 1872. In addition, the development in Germany differed in that it was not the textile industry, but the coal, iron and steel industries and railway construction that became the key industries. Away from these centres, for example in Holzminden, development was even slower. Haarmann's foundation in 1874 actually coincided with the phase of high industrialisation in the German Empire.

However, the chemical industry was also a fairly new industry that was dependent on the increase in knowledge and the number of graduates in chemistry. Between 1860 and 1900, both the number of companies in the chemical industry and their size grew rapidly. For example, Badische Anilin- und Sodafabrik (BASF – Baden Aniline and Soda Factory), founded in 1865, already employed 2,330 workers and employees in 1885. This increased to 4,600 in 1895 and 6,711 in 1900. At Bayer/Elberfeld, founded in 1863, there were initially 24 chemists and 300 workers in 1885. By 1896 there were 104 chemists and 2,644 workers.

At the time, the chemical industry was seen as a force for peace and, thus, a safeguard for the State. Fertilisers and pesticides were used to increase agricultural yields. Dyes and pigments provided colours for clothing, printed matter and house façades. Synthetic fibres made textiles cheaper, and plastics brought new goods for households and industry. Medicines improved health and reduced the risk of infection from dangerous and contagious diseases. However, the use of poison gas during the First World War and visible environmental damage soon changed this positive picture.

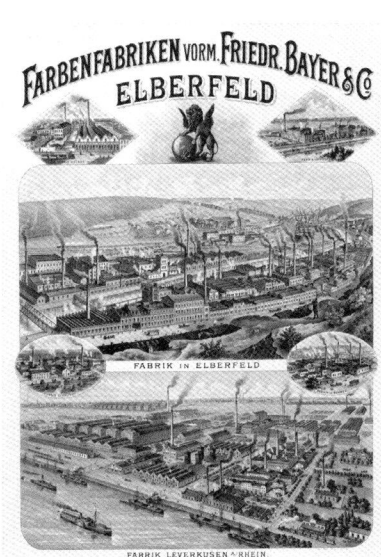

The Bayer factory site in 1895

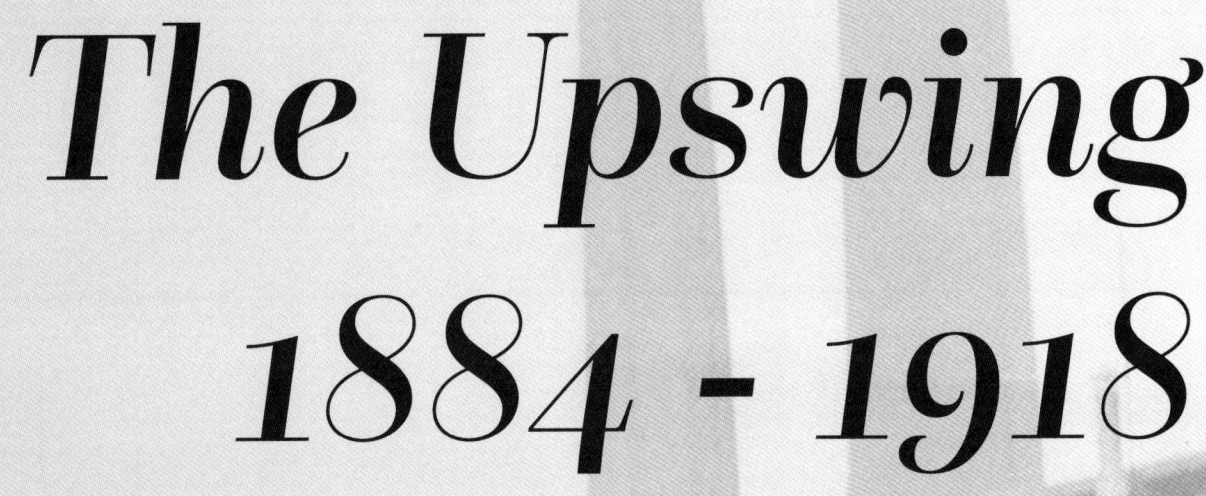

The Upswing
1884 - 1918

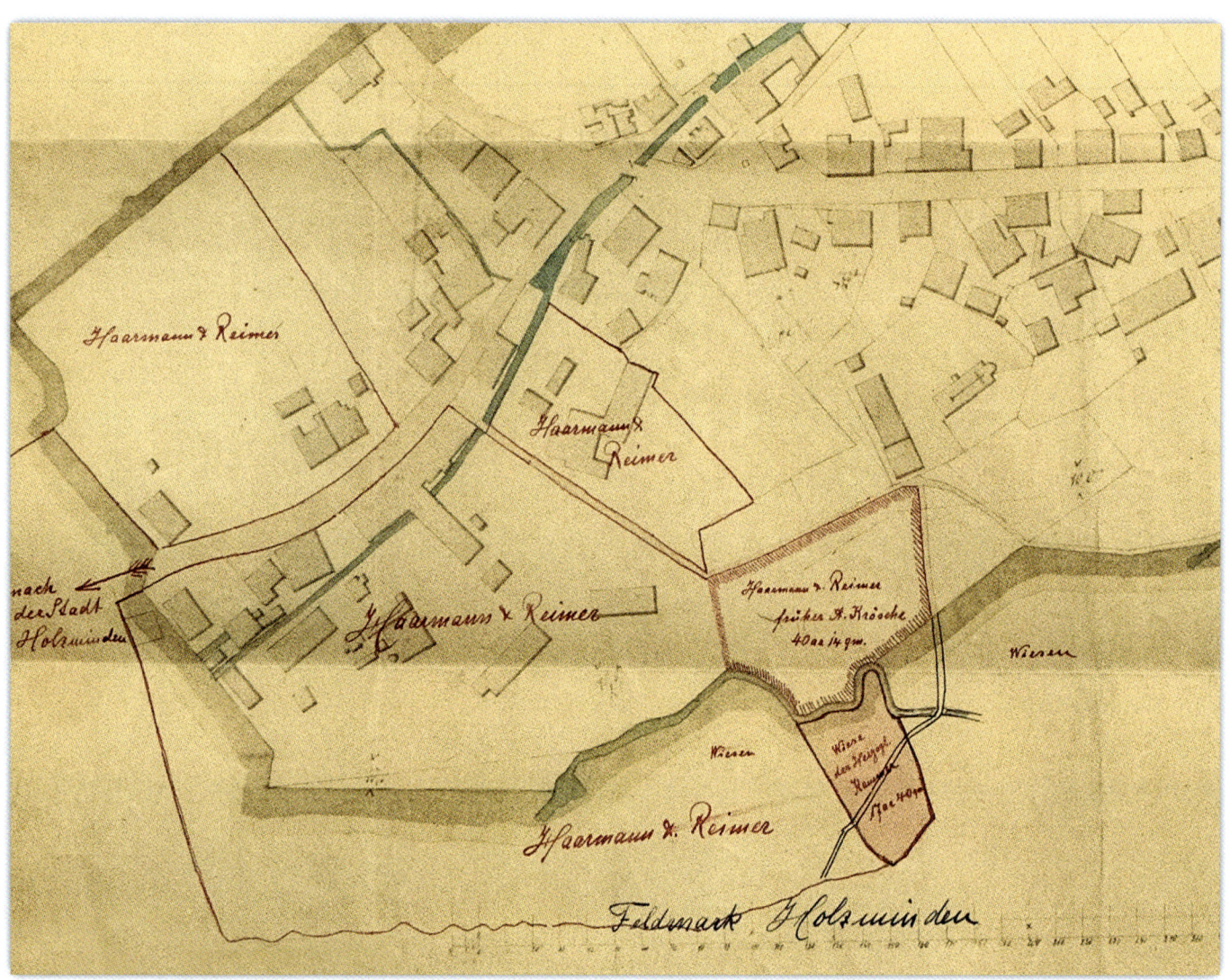

This map of Altendorf from the 1890s shows that Haarmann & Reimer had expanded the company premises in various directions.

In the early years, Haarmann & Reimer's business was probably only able to survive with the financial support of Wilhelm Haarmann's father and the Nolda family, who were distantly related. Added to this was the founders' unshakeable belief in the company's success. From the mid-1880s, profits were finally being generated. However, other chemical companies had also recognised the opportunities that lay in the synthetic production of vanilla flavouring. With the expiry of the first vanillin patents and the development of alternative synthesis methods for obtaining vanillin, various German, Swiss and French chemical manufacturers began producing vanillin.

1886 – Vanillin-Convention

In order to force the competition out of the market and prevent a further fall in the price of vanillin, Wilhelm Haarmann approached a number of strong competitors. Business cartels did not have a bad reputation back then. In the Ruhr region, for example, the Rhenish-Westphalian Coal Syndicate and the Rhenish-Westphalian Pig Iron Syndicate were formed through the amalgamation of coal mines and ironworks. Price agreements were considered a tried and tested means of entrepreneurial behaviour: in 1886, C. F. Boehringer & Söhne, Mannheim; E. Schering; Schimmel & Co; and Haarmann & Reimer negotiated a Vanillin Convention with price agreements. Wilhelm Haarmann's company chronicle reads: "… heavy levies to the competition …". The Vanillin Convention secured the market power of the participating companies. However, the fixed prices were low in order to force other suppliers out of the market and to prevent potential competitors from investing in expensive production facilities. However, this was also felt by the participating companies themselves.

In the early years, Haarmann & Reimer tried to sell vanillin and vanillin sugar in ready-to-use packets directly to the consumer. This is evidenced by numerous advertisements in various daily newspapers in the 1880s and 1890s.

1887 – First chocolate vending machines

Vanilla-flavoured chocolate had been a sought-after and valuable product since the middle of the 19th century and was an important sales market for the use of inexpensive vanillin. However, the Association of German Chocolate Manufacturers initially had reservations about the artificial flavouring. Tiemann and Haarmann, therefore, travelled to the chocolate manufacturers' association meetings to promote their product. In the end, it was probably the significantly more favourable price that won them over. And, thus, chocolate became a mass-produced item. As early as 1887, the Cologne confectionery producer Ludwig Stollwerck set up the first chocolate vending machines and with immense success: by 1890, Stollwerck had already sold 18 million bars in this way.

Stollwerck was very successful with chocolate vending machines which was also made possible by a decrease in the production costs of chocolate.

1884 – 1918

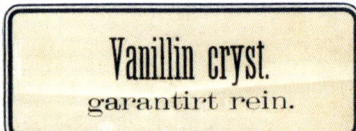

Labels and trademarks c.1900

1888 – New chemists arrived to expand the product range

Presumably through Tiemann's influence, further chemists from the Chemical Institute of Berlin joined Haarmann & Reimer to drive forward the development of new fragrances and flavourings. Dr. P. Krüger arrived in 1888 and devoted himself to the development of terpineol and ionone amongst others. Dr. Sembritzki and Dr. Schmidt followed in 1891. Dr. Lemme joined in 1893, and, finally, Dr. Kerschbaum in 1897.

This significantly expanded the company's product range in the 1890s and is evidenced by the 30 patents that Haarmann & Reimer registered internationally between 1893 and 1903.

Although there were further advances in vanillin production, the lucrative trade margin and high demand meant that competition on the vanillin market was very strong, reducing the profit margin in this area.

1890 – Construction of a villa in Höxter

From 1876 to 1884, Wilhelm Haarmann lived at Bahnhofstrasse 6 in the very house in which Carl Wilhelm Gerberding would found the fragrance company Dragoco 35 years later. The house was destroyed in a bombing raid in 1945. From 1885, the young Haarmann family lived at Allersheimer Strasse 3, their second house. This house also no longer exists as it had to make way for the new police station in the 1980s. However, the Haarmanns had already moved out in 1890 and relocated to

Dr Max Kerschbaum in the laboratory

Dr Paul Krüger

Dr Semberitzki

Dr Richard Schmidt

Dr Lemme

1884 – 1918

Villa Haarmann under construction, as seen from the Rodeneck Tower, which Höxter. Wilhelm Haarmann had purchased an attractive plot of land with a view of the Weser on the slope of the Ziegenberg outside the old town centre and had had an Italian-style villa built.

Villa Haarmann after completion

Workers' Houses in Liebigstraße

Haarmann also started building projects in Holzminden. In the same year, he had workers' houses built in Liebigstrasse not far from the factory premises. These semi-detached houses were each equipped with stables and a quarter of an acre of land to enable self-sufficiency. It can be assumed that the workers were semi-skilled, former farm labourers. In the agricultural region, there were only a few industrial companies from which the vanillin factory could have poached its labour. In addition, the chemical industry was a completely new branch of industry with previously unknown activities. From 1865 to 1871, the population of Holzminden rose from 4,788 to 5,932, and the town experienced a certain economic upswing after being connected to the railway network. In any case, it was certainly difficult for ordinary labourers to find affordable housing. By building the workers' houses, Haarmann & Reimer not only provided relief for the workers, but also bound the workers and their families to the factory, as it would have been very difficult to find replacements for experienced workers in Holzminden. As can be seen from some documents (for example, the visit of the Regent in 1909), Wilhelm Haarmann cultivated a patriarchal and friendly relationship with his workers. They, in turn, thanked him with great loyalty.

Workers' houses built by Haarmann & Reimer in Liebigstrasse

Exact records have not been preserved for Haarmann & Reimer, but, in 1874, the working week was around 68 hours, and, in 1890, it was still 66 hours on six days, i.e. more than ten hours a day. As early as 1877, employers founded the Association for the Protection of the Interests of the Chemical Industry in Germany, but it was not until 13 years later, on 1 July 1890 at the congress of all non-industrial workers in Germany, that unskilled workers from various places in the German Empire came together in Hannover to establish the Association of Factory, Agricultural and Industrial Auxiliary Workers in Germany, the predecessor organisation of the Chemical, Paper and Ceramic Workers' Trade Union, which was founded in 1946. According to its statutes, the association accepted all workers *"who do not work in a specific trade and all industrial workers who are unable to join their professional organisations due to local circumstances"*. These were primarily workers in the emerging branches of industry, such as the chemical, rubber and paper-producing industries. By the beginning of the First World War, the trade unions in the German Empire had succeeded in reducing the working week by more than ten hours to an average of 55 hours. The factory workers' association also drew attention to the dangers of accidents and toxic substances in the chemical industry and achieved numerous improvements in working conditions.

A double page from the guide to the German chemical industry exhibition at the World's Columbian Exposition in Chicago 1893.

1893 – World's Columbian Exposition

After the 1876 World Exhibition in Philadelphia had first showcased North America's industrial prowess, the USA presented itself in Chicago in 1893, 400 years after the discovery of America by Columbus, on a scale which had not been seen before: 70,000 exhibitors from 46 countries presented themselves on 81 hectares in architecturally impressive halls, pavilions and carefully designed open spaces. Haarmann & Reimer also exhibited at the World's Columbian Exposition in Chicago in 1893. In addition to vanillin, more than 20 other artificial fragrances were exhibited. The first artificial violet odourant, ionone, developed by Tiemann in collaboration with P. Krüger and patented by Haarmann & Reimer in 1893, was particularly prominent. Like vanillin, ionones are still among the most important fragrances in perfumery today.

In connection with the world exhibition, we also learn something about the corporate culture at Haarmann & Reimer. The guide states, among other things: "*The factory takes the greatest possible care of the welfare of the workers it employs, who receive a daily wage of 250 - 390 Pf. for ten hours' work.*" Haarmann & Reimer was apparently a comparatively good employer for its 39 workers, four chemists and three administrative staff. According to the German Bundesbank's purchasing power parity table, this daily wage is equivalent to three to four euros today.

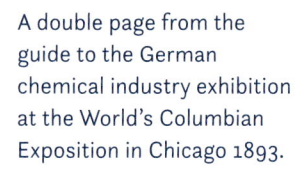

Suits and cigars: in the 19th century, chemists in Haarmann & Reimer's laboratories did not yet wear white coats.

The Upswing

1895 – Battle for the vanillin market

Despite the many product developments, the vanillin business remained the main source of income, and it remained highly competitive. To keep the competition on the vanillin market in check, Wilhelm Haarmann did more than just set up a cartel. In 1895, Haarmann & Reimer entered into a licence agreement with the Gesellschaft für Chemische Industrie (Society for the Chemical Industry) in Basel. The company had invented an effective process for the production of vanillin, the practical application of which Haarmann & Reimer secured by paying a fee of 80,000 marks per year. In this way, 2,000 kg of vanillin were produced in Holzminden each year for many years. By way of comparison, the production quantities of vanillin were seven kilograms in 1874 and 80 kilograms in 1875.

1895 – Lina Morgenstern's vanillin recipe book

Despite all the success, the general public still had reservations about the artificial flavouring vanillin. To overcome this, Haarmann & Reimer and the well-known recipe book author Lina Morgenstern published the recipe book *Kochrezepte mit Anwendung von Haarmann & Reimers Patent. Vanillin* (Recipes Using Haarmann & Reimer's Patented Vanillin). The compact and inexpensive publication contained 39 recipes ranging from chocolate soup to vanilla compôtes. The foreword "For the discerning housewife" states: "*Vanilla is one of the finest, tastiest and most flavourful spices, which is why the finer art of cooking uses it in the most varied ways. In middle-class cuisine, on the other hand, vanilla has not yet earned its rightful place, even though it adds flavour to simple milk soup and the cheapest pastries.*"

It continues that the "*fruit from the tropics is difficult to preserve*", challenging and expensive but now vanilla would be available as a

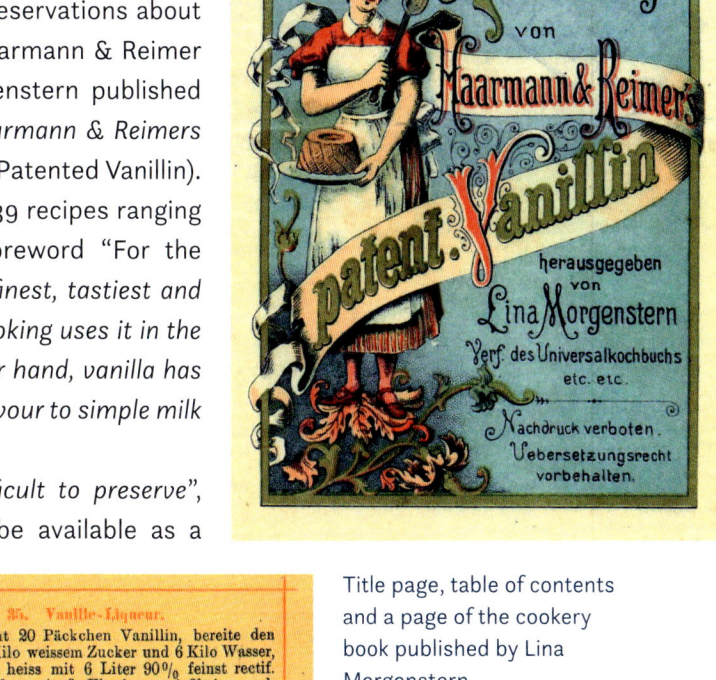

Title page, table of contents and a page of the cookery book published by Lina Morgenstern

Correspondence with Schimmel & Co

1896 January 28[?]
Schimmel & Co, Leipzig, to Haarmann & Reimer, Holzminden
"We received your esteemed letter dated 24th with a sample of vanillin-Böhringer, which we have carefully examined and unfortunately have to classify as completely unusable.
It looks good on the outside, but when dissolved it has a penetrating smell of guaiacol or creosol. When mixed with excess sodium bisulphite solution, the vanillin smell disappears completely and only the smell of the phenols mentioned remains.

We commend ourselves to you
Yours respectfully!
Schimmel & Co"

This letter from Schimmel & Co proves that the two specialist companies in fragrance chemistry were already in contact with each other in the 19th century. It is reasonable to assume that Schimmel & Co and Haarmann & Reimer had to show a sense of solidarity in the face of the large-scale chemical industry, which in this case was represented by Böhringer.

domestic product: "*Not that we can pick the ripe vanilla pods in our climate, but through the important invention of two German researchers, Dr. W. Haarmann in Holzminden and Professor Dr. Ferd. Tiemann at the Royal University of Berlin, the body of the vanilla, which alone produces the aroma of the vanilla pod, can be artificially created from readily accessible natural materials. What brittle nature has denied us in our latitudes, the researcher wrests from it in a fervent desire for knowledge.*"

Haarmann & Reimer addressed end consumers directly here because "*for household use, the patent holders combine vanillin with sugar in a very specific ratio, put it into handy sachets that correspond exactly to the effect of a stick of fine vanilla, and market them for household use.*"

Hence, Haarmann & Reimer was the first supplier of the vanillin sugar sachets that are so successful today. But despite all its endeavours, it was not successful with this product. Instead, the company Dr. Oetker, founded in Bielefeld in 1891, succeeded a few years later. The food manufacturer, which had emerged from a pharmacy, obviously enjoyed more trust than the chemical factory. In addition, the vanilla sugar packaged in small sachets built on the success of Dr. Oetker baking powder. Dr. Oetker began industrial production around 1900 and its main suppliers were the companies Boehringer Mannheim, and Schering.

Nevertheless, the vanillin business was a success for Haarmann & Reimer. Sales figures for vanillin are available for the period from October to December 1895: 502 kg of vanillin was sold in those three months, 22% of which was sold on the American market.

Advertisement from 1892

Patent disputes

Haarmann & Reimer had quickly lost its unique selling point when it came to vanillin, but the company's products were apparently still superior in quality to those of its competitors, so that Haarmann & Reimer's vanillin was able to hold its own on the market.

In the 1890s, numerous new fragrances were synthesised in Haarmann & Reimer's laboratories. Here, too, the competition saw the potential and rushed to bring these substances onto the market as well.

As patent law in Germany then only protected the new manufacturing process and not the newly obtained substance itself, Tiemann and Haarmann had to prove that the same production method was actually being used if they wanted to take action against imitation.

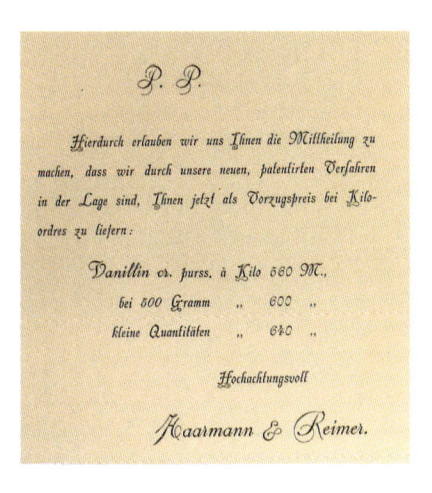

Preferential price for vanillin: 560 marks a kilogramme in 1895

Handwritten list from the 1890s with the due dates of various patents in different countries.

Top right: a warning letter regarding the production of ionone in violation of patent law. The letter reveals that the product is being distributed not only by Haarmann & Reimer and de Laire & Co. but also by Schimmel & Co in Leipzig.

The ionone trial

The so-called ionone trial took place before a court in Hamburg between Haarmann & Reimer and Fritsche, from Hamburg. It concerned the synthetic violet fragrance and even attracted international attention. The trial dragged on for years but Haarmann & Reimer was able to win because the opposing side had been careless when filing the patent application in England. The future Nobel Prize winner Adolf von Baeyer acted as an expert witness for Haarmann & Reimer.

However, other lawsuits were lost because the court did not recognise the evidence or expert opinions submitted by Haarmann & Reimer. Ferdinand Tiemann had campaigned especially for the enforcement of the Haarmann & Reimer patents. The numerous nerve-wracking trials, at which he often had to appear in person, apparently damaged his health. After an exhausting court hearing in London, he suffered a serious heart attack on his return to Berlin in July 1899.

1899 – Ferdinand Tiemann's death

Following his heart attack, Ferdinand Tiemann spent time at a health resort in Merano, but even this could not save his life. He died in the sanatorium on 14 November 1899 at the age of just 51. In 1901, Otto Nikolaus Witt wrote in his detailed obituary of Ferdinand Tiemann in the Reports of the German Chemical Society: "*With the expansion of the chemistry of the citral and ionone group, Tiemann had accomplished the most brilliant, but also the last work of his life, which was so rich in labour. The surprising technical success of this brilliant achievement was to be his undoing. [...] Here, too, the patent protection he obtained proved to be insufficient to maintain the exclusive ownership of intellectual property rightly claimed by its inventor. The violet fragrance has always been the most expensive of all fragrances.*" The "great abundance" of the synthetic fragrance made it possible to market the product at prices "*many times higher than that of gold - so it was no wonder that the competitors in the Holzminden and Paris factories used every means at their disposal to produce the precious fragrance in secret or blatant violation [...] of the ionone patent. [...] The fight against the unlawful producers and sellers of ionone began, a battle which our friend - unfortunately - reserved the right to organise and personally lead. This battle wore him out.*"

Ferdinand Tiemann was born in Rübeland am Harz, first moving to Brunswick and then to Berlin to study. As an antithesis to life in the city, he evidently also felt happy, perhaps even at home, in the Solling forest near Holzminden. In his obituary, Otto Nikolaus Witt writes in another place: "*The writer of these lines remembers with pleasure some of the summer days he spent with his departed friend in and near Holzminden. A sunny cheerfulness, a comfortable feeling of freedom seemed to come over him; he knew every flower we encountered on our walks through the woods.*"

However, Tiemann's time spent in the countryside was probably rather rare as his work at the company and at the Friedrich Wilhelm University of Berlin, which appointed him professor in 1878, kept him too busy. In addition to his intensive scientific work in the laboratory, he also worked for 24 years as secretary of the *Berichte der Deutschen Chemischen Gesellschaft* (Reports of the German Chemical Society), and 15 years as editor. This also earned him recognition among the scientific community.

Drawing from 1898 by O. N. Witt, then President of the German Chemical Society, with the text:
*This is St. Ferdinand
He is known throughout the empire
Pray to him for a while!
He will put you in good aroma.
And give you enough of the sweet scents of roses, lilies and violets*

This postcard from 1903 shows the view from above the middle pond, with the weir of the upper pond and the sandstone grinding mill on the right and the Haarmann & Reimann factory in the background.

1884 – 1918

1899 – Haarmann & Reimer expands its premises

Until now Haarmann & Reimer's factory buildings had stretched along the street known today as An den Teichen above the upper pond. It was located only in the area of Altendorf which was an independent village at that time. The pond supplied water to drive the stone grinding mills of the Administration of the Solling Sandstone Quarries directly below it and also to the linen bleachers called Hühn which were situated on the south of the pond. To extend the company premises, Haarmann & Reimer purchased the adjoining Hofmann farmstead, which had an area of 25,000 square metres, in the east of Altendorf in 1899. The residential buildings were converted into two workers' flats. In the following year, Haarmann & Reimer received the first telephone line, number 19. An American subsidiary was also founded; Haarmann-de Laire-Schaefer Company in Maywood in New Jersey.

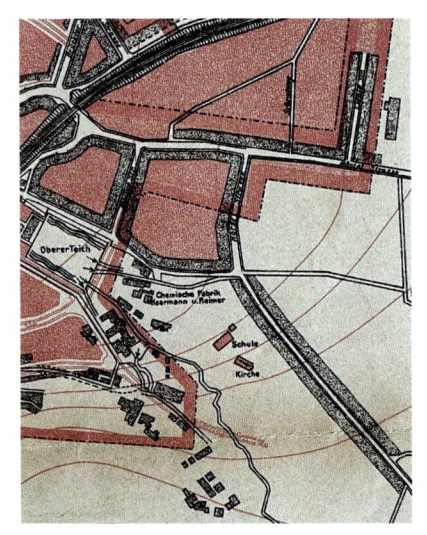

Idealised drawing of the Haarmann & Reimer premises

Section of a city map from 1908

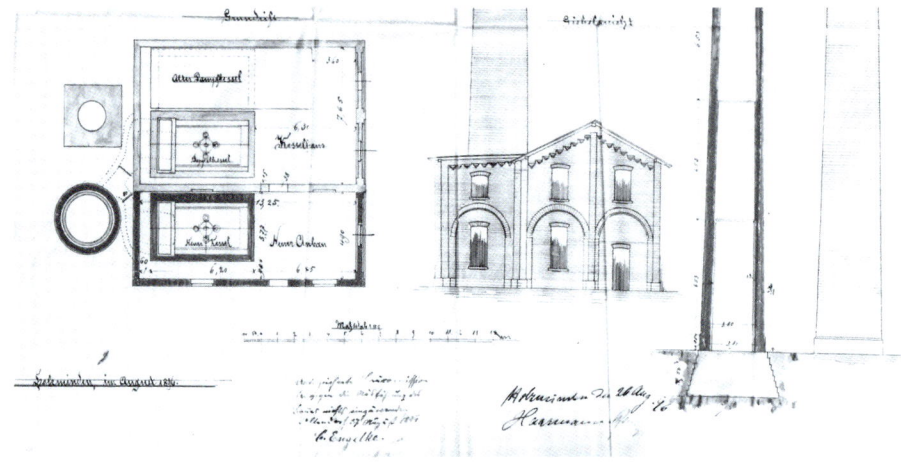

Top right: blueprint for the new boiler house from 1896

Below: view of the boiler house c.1920

The Upswing

Above: company premises from the east

Left: in the Haarmann & Reimer boiler house, which is located in the building on the left in the picture above.

Below: view from the south over Fabrikstrasse, and beyond it, the company grounds of Haarmann & Reimer, which are surrounded by a wall.

1900 – World Exhibition in Paris

With 48 million visitors, the World Exhibition in Paris was one of the most successful exhibitions of its kind and was to mark a turning point at the beginning of the 20th century. In a state decree on the exhibition, the French Minister of Trade and Industry wrote: "*It should mark the end of a fruitful century and show what art and science and human labour are capable of creating; but it should also become the threshold of a new age, of which scholars and philosophers prophesise great things, and whose creative power will exceed all our dreams and expectations.*" Haarmann & Reimer was represented as part of the "*Collective Exhibition of the German Chemical Industry*". In the catalogue, after the presentation of products and research achievements, social aspects are discussed in considerable detail: "*The company is located in Altendorf near Holzminden and employs 8 technical clerks, 5 merchants and 65 labourers. [...] The company provides numerous welfare facilities for its workers. [...] Hot coffee is served twice a day. At Christmas, gifts and savings deposits are distributed.*"

The following is noted about the history: "*The business gradually developed into a factory of artificial fragrances of all kinds, which are presented and introduced onto the market in a state of perfect purity.*"

Description of the company in the catalogue for the "collective exhibition of the German chemical industry" at the World Exhibition in Paris.

1901 – Haarmann & Reimer becomes a 'GmbH' and a Holzminden company

Strictly speaking, Haarmann & Reimer was a company in the village of Altendorf until the turn of the century. Although this village was located in the immediate vicinity to the east of the town of Holzminden, it was independent until 1921. Haarmann & Reimer's first production facilities were located in Altendorf. In 1901, Haarmann & Reimer then acquired directly neighbouring areas of the town of Holzminden. In October 1901, the company was also converted into a limited liability company: "*The object of the company is the takeover and continuation of the limited partnership Haarmann & Reimer, which has existed in Holzminden since 20 May 1891, together with the company name, the chemical manufacturing and trading business operating under this name with assets and liabilities, the enlargement and expansion of this factory, the acquisition and operation of other chemical factories and all other chemical manufacturing and trading businesses, and participation in other similar companies.*

Postcard of Altendorf with a view of the vanillin factory (c.1900, photographer: Otto Liebert)

The Upswing

Coloured photo of the company premises at the upper pond, c.1920

The company's share capital amounts to 449,800 marks. Dr. Wilhelm Haarmann of Höxter is appointed managing director, and Dr. Richard Schmidt and Dr. Ferdinand Sembritzki are appointed deputy managing directors.
[...]
With the exception of the cash investments, the partners' investments are realised by each of the partners contributing their entire share in the previous limited partnership to the limited liability company. The value of these shares is:

1. for Dr. Wilhelm Haarmann 82,500 M.
2. for the heirs of Professor Dr. Ferdinand Tiemann in Berlin, [...] 82,500 M,
3. for Edgar de Laire in Paris: 82,500 M,
4. for merchant Alfred Max in Paris: 21,000 M.,
5. for merchant Eugene Max in Paris: 15,700 M.,
6. for merchant Charles Max in Paris: 15,700 M."

Haarmann & Reimer's premises, thus, extended as far as Fabrikstrasse where Pistorius iron foundry, Dr Abbes pulley factory, Steinmeier paper factory, Bertling vinegar factory, a timber saccharification plant, a linen bleaching plant and other businesses had settled. Haarmann & Reimer also received access to the railway via Fabrikstrasse.

Schematic plan of the company premises in 1909, with a railway siding on Fabrikstrasse

1884 – 1918

Verzeichnis der von Haarmann & Reimer am 14. November 1903 an die C o m m i s s i o n zur Vorbereitung der Chemischen Ausstellung auf der deutschen Unterrichts-Ausstellung zu St. Louis 1904, Berlin N.W., Invalidenstrasse, Landesausstellungs-Palast, gesandten Präparate:

	Name	Gewicht	Jahr der Entdeckung	Wert
1.)	Coniferin	100 Gramm	1866	M. 15.--
2.)	Eugenol	230 "	1834	" 3.50
3.)	Isoeugenol	230 "	1882	" 4.50
4.)	Vanillin	120 "	1874	" 6.--
5.)	Vanillinsäure	120 "	1875	" 12.--
6.)	Piperin	150 "	1855	" 11.--
7.)	Piperinsäure	100 "	1857	" 18.--
8.)	Safrol	230 "	1869	" --.70
9.)	Isosafrol	230 "	1890	" 1.80
10.)	Heliotropin (Piperonal)	120 "	1869	" 2.40
11.)	Piperonylsäure	120 "	1869	" 12.--
12.)	Protocatecusäure	100 "	1869	" 20.--
13.)	Salicylaldehyd	200 "	1839	" 6.--
14.)	Cumarin	150 "	1859	" 4.50
15.)	p.Oxybenzaldehyd	100 "	1876	" 10.--
16.)	Anisaldehyd	200 "	1845	" 8.--
17.)	Anethol	200 "	1842	" 4.--
18.)	Anissäure	100 "	1842	" 4.--
19.)	Geraniol	230 "	1871	" 6.--
20.)	Citral	230 Gramm	1890	M. 8.--
21.)	Cyclocitral	230 "	1898	" 110.--
22.)	Methylheptenon	230 "	1890	" 20.--
23.)	Linalool	230 "	1891	" 7.--
24.)	Linalylacetat	230 "	1891	" 16.--
25.)	Citronellol	230 "	1896	" 60.--
26.)	Citronellal	230 "	1875	" 7.--
27.)	Iridin	100 "	1893	" 10.--
28.)	Iron	230 "	1893	" 200.--
29.)	Jonon	230 "	1893	" 200.--
30.)	Jonon	230 "	1893	" 200.--

In 1903, Haarmann & Reimer presented numerous products at the World Exhibition in St. Louis, USA. An accompanying letter to Dr. Marwedel from Haarmann-de Laire-Schaefer Company states: "*You, hereby, receive a further sample collection of our products. We would kindly ask you to discuss with Dr. Schaefer and Dodge & Olcott which of these products could be of interest to America.*"

1909 – The Regent's visit

During his sightseeing tour through the Brunswick Weser district, Brunswick Regent Johann Albrecht Duke of Mecklenburg stopped at Haarmann & Reimer, which had gained significance in the Duchy of Brunswick primarily due to its international operations. In addition to Haarmann & Reimer, the Regent also visited the private school currently under construction and the Allersheim brewery, where he drank a glass of beer "*with pleasure and appreciation*". The report on the visit continues: "*The sales areas [of H&R] extend across all recognised countries. Because of the high American customs duties, the company felt compelled to set up a branch in New York.*"

Haarmann & Reimer now employed 7 chemists, 9 commercial and administrative staff, 1 electrical engineer and 60 labourers.

In 1909, the management and chemists of Haarmann & Reimer dressed in top hat and tails for the Regent's visit. Wilhelm Haarmann's note, dated 18 June 1909, inviting everyone concerned to "*beer and open sandwiches*" shows that the visit was to everyone's satisfaction.

Haarmann & Reimer,
CHEMISCHE FABRIK ZU HOLZMINDEN, G. M. B. H.

CONTO BEI DER DEUTSCHEN BANK, BERLIN.
POSTSCHECK-CONTO No. 299 HANNOVER.

TELEPHON No. 19.
LIEBER'S CODE USED.

Holzminden, den 18. Juni 1909.

    Ich habe mich gefreut, dass alle nach ihren besten Kräften dazu beigetragen haben, dass ich die Fabrik dem Herzog-Regenten in tadellosem Zustande habe vorführen können. Se Hoheit hat sich sehr anerkennend über das Gesehene geäussert, und spreche ich allen meinen Dank für ihre Mitwirkung aus.

    Sämtliche in der Fabrik Beschäftigte lade ich auf Sonnabend Abend ½8 - ½11 Uhr zu einem Glase Bier und Butterbrot nach Heller's Gastwirtschaft ein.

Dr. Wilh. Haarmann

1909 – The year of the lily-of-the-valley

In his fundamental essay on The Development Of The Essential Oil Industry Over The Last 25 Years, the chemist Albert Hesse writes: *"In the anniversary year of 1909, the company Haarmann & Reimer, whose endeavours supported by Tiemann were ground-breaking for the production of individual fragrances, [...] achieved a wonderful success in the field of complex fragrances by producing an artificial lily-of-the-valley oil. This delicate perfume has been received with such enthusiasm by a public weary of the intrusive, intense perfumes of recent years that 1909 can rightly be described as the year of the lily-of-the-valley from a perfumery point of view."*

Albert Hesse also wrote about Haarmann & Reimer's research, stating that the invention of ionone had brought about a "tremendous turnaround in perfumery and in the assessment of artificial fragrances by perfumers".

Steamboat trip to Bodenwerder, 14 June 1913: a Haarmann & Reimer company outing

Ethyl Vanillin

Ethyl vanillin was discovered at Haarmann & Reimer before the First World War and launched under the name Bourbanol. In chemical terms, the methyl group of ethyl vanillin is exchanged for an ethyl group. The substance is two to four times more intense than vanillin, but does not occur naturally. For this reason, ethyl vanillin was, initially, only allowed to be used in perfumery.

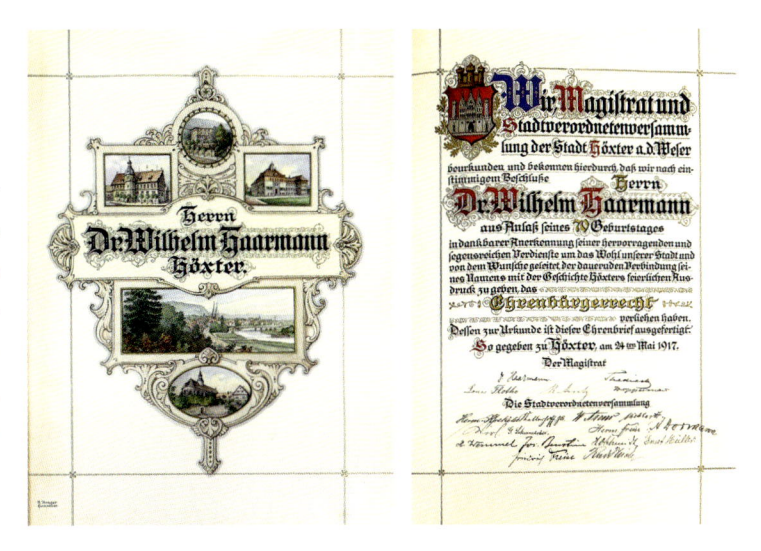

On his 70th birthday, the town of Höxter honoured Wilhelm Haarmann with honorary citizenship *"in grateful recognition of his outstanding and beneficial services to the well-being of our town"*.

The chemical industry in the First World War

A very dark chapter in the history of chemistry started to unfold during the First World War. With the production and first use of poison gas in April 1915, Germany 'opened' the gas war with the active help of the chemical industry which also helped the German Reich to produce explosives by synthesising ammonia using the Haber-Bosch process. Saltpetre deliveries were suspended quite early due to the British naval blockade. The shortage of explosives should probably have led to a much earlier end to the war.

Although the patents for ammonia production had to be surrendered by BASF after the end of the war in accordance with the Treaty of Versailles, BASF and later I.G. Farben (Dye Industry Syndicate) remained the world's largest producer of ammonia which was mainly used for fertiliser in agriculture.

Overall, the German chemical industry experienced an upswing during the First World War due to the factors mentioned above. Despite the reparations stipulated in the Treaty of Versailles, the technical production expertise and most of the production facilities were preserved. During the war the companies had to adhere to the requirements of the state's planned economy but after the war they were able to push ahead with the development of new substances and expand their production of profitable products. Domestic inflation proved to be a definite advantage in the export sector.

In the years that followed, the major chemical manufacturers also discovered the lucrative fragrance market thanks to the potential of their production facilities and access to raw materials, and, thus, began competing with specialists such as Haarmann & Reimer.

In 1912, Carl Duisberg was appointed general director and chairman of the board of Farbenfabriken vorm. Friedr. Bayer & Co. (Dye Factories, formerly Friedr. Bayer & Co.) Duisberg was one of the most important advocates of the use of poison gas in the First World War: *"This chloric carbon oxide is the most terrible stuff I know. [...] But the only appropriate place to try something like this is at the front, and there won't be another opportunity anytime soon in the future to do so either. [...] I can, therefore, only once again urgently recommend not to let the opportunity of this war pass by without also testing the poison gas grenade."*

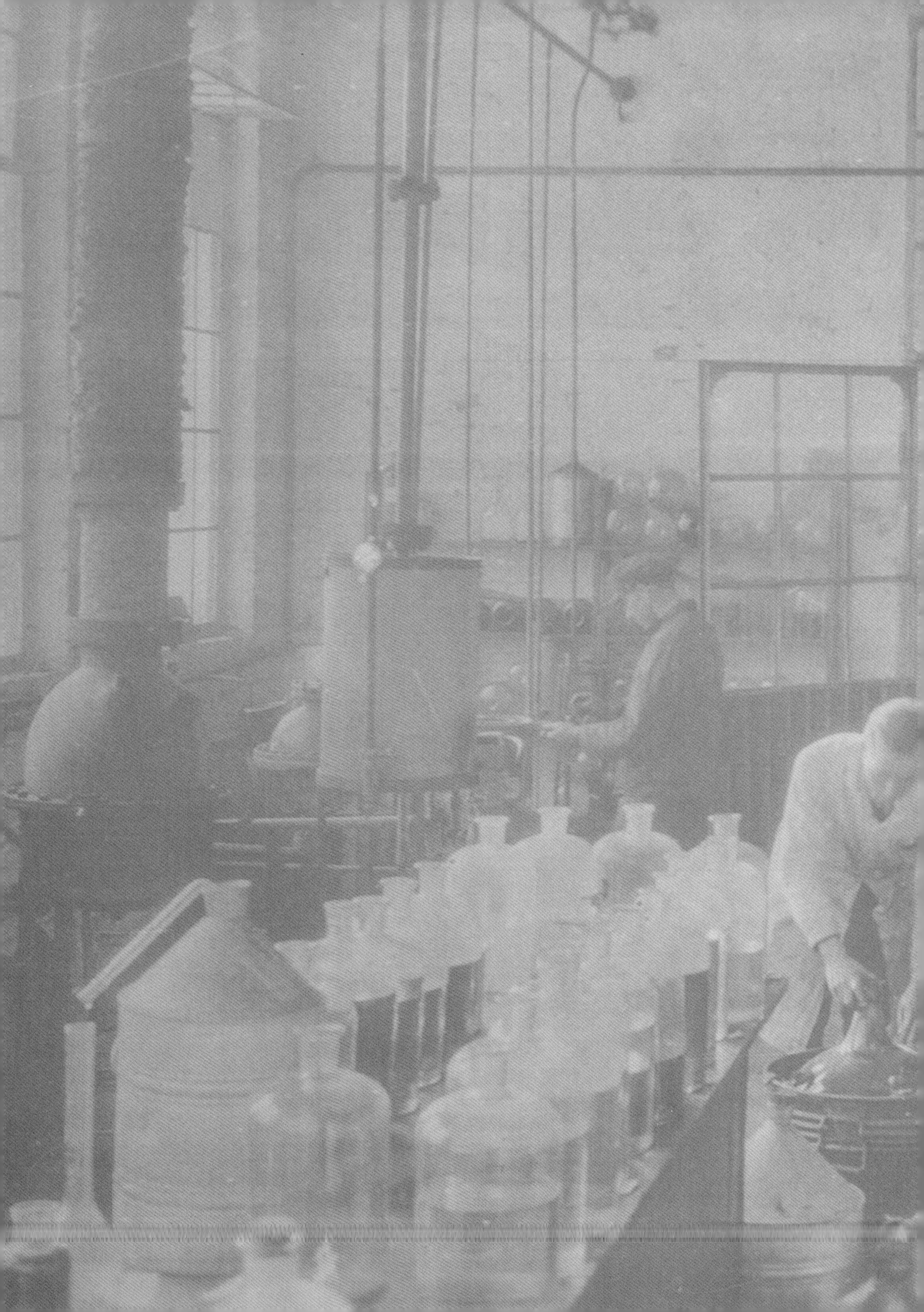

New Beginnings and Another War
1919 - 1945

Bahnhofstrasse 6: the birthplace of Carl-Wilhelm Gerberding. It was during the First World War in his mother's hairdressing salon that Gerberding first experimented with hair tonics and perfumes and where he founded his company immediately after the War.
In April 1945, the building was hit by a bomb and destroyed.

New Beginnings ...

Im During the First World War, only Haarmann & Reimer and Boehringer Mannheim were able to maintain the production of vanillin. The economic blockade by the Allies hit the economy hard and total production fell. However, as many fragrances and flavourings were lacking on the German market, the importance of vanillin as a food flavouring grew.
Compared to many other substitutes, synthetic vanillin was only slightly inferior to the natural flavour of vanilla which meant that many concerns about this synthetic product disappeared. The repeated press reports about vanillin poisoning also proved to be untenable and on closer examination, the cause of the poisoning was always the actual food (ice cream or custard) and not the extremely low doses of the flavouring agent.

This will have been one of the reasons why the globally-active company hardly suffered any lasting damage despite all the temporary restrictions. However, Haarmann & Reimer lost its stake in its French partner company De Laire & Co, while that company was able to retain the shares in the German company. In addition, the lack of supplies from German companies during the First World War led to the emergence of rival companies in other European countries. As vanillin had, meanwhile, been detected in other plant species and also in the waste water of cellulose factories, various new methods for vanillin production had also been developed. In 1926, there were 18 companies producing vanillin worldwide, including the companies of the Vanillin Convention in Germany.

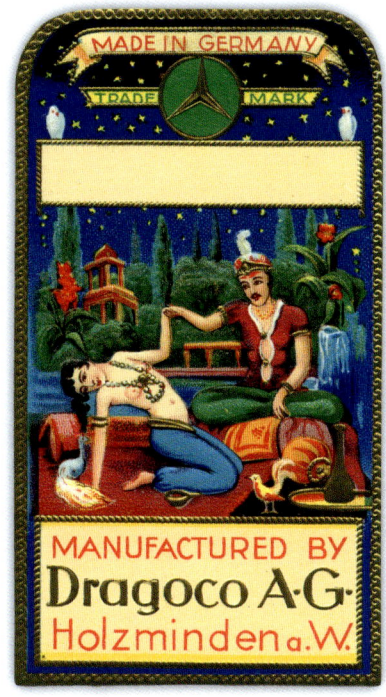

The label from Dragoco's early days emphasises the international aspirations of the newly established company in Holzminden.

1919 – Founding of the Drago Works

A new company was also established in Holzminden after the war: Carl Wilhelm Gerberding, the son of a master hairdresser, founded Drago-Werke, chemische Fabrik (Drago-Works, Chemical Factory) in Holzminden together with his cousin August Bellmer. The company produced hair tonics as well as perfume and soap compositions. The company name stems from dragon reflecting Gerberding's love of the Far East and its ancient fragrance culture. Gerberding later designed the logo with the Asian-style dragon himself.

The company headquarters were located in his parents' house in Bahnhofstrasse. Legend has it that Gerberding mixed his first creations in a bathtub. His father had passed away in 1908 and the hairdressing business was leased out with his mother running the adjoining 'bathing establishment'. Carl-Heinz Gerberding (son of the company founder) wrote in his memoirs that his grandmother prepared the baths herself *"normal or with the fragrance of pine. It was a green oil that not only coloured the water green, but also emanated powerful spruce forest scents. Normal cost 25 Pf, pine scent 40 Pf. Grandmother, therefore, used the pine scent sparingly. If the successor to a spruce bath also wanted one, the tub was not drained completely, but simply refilled. That saved 'green' oil."*

The year in which Dragoco was founded (Drago-Werke was renamed Dragoco a few years after being established) may seem strange at first glance: after the First World War, there was great hardship in Germany and political chaos in spite of the Republic having been proclaimed at the end of 1918. On the other hand,

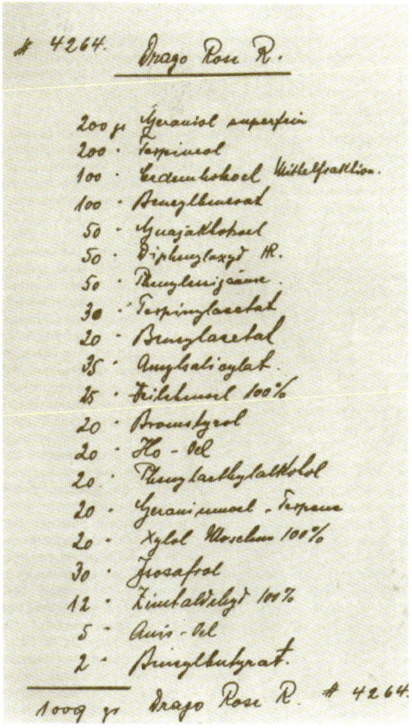

Formula handwritten by Carl Wilhelm Gerberding

1919 – 1945

Liste der wahlberechtigten Arbeiter 1923.

Lfd. Nr.	Namen	Lfd. Nr.	Namen	Lfd. Nr.	Namen
1.	Schutz	26.	Klages 1	51.	Schwarze
2.	Riegling	27.	Kreikenbohm	52.	Henze
3.	Kramer	28.	Hilmer 1	53.	Timmermann 1
4.	Heise I	29.	Mahlmann	54.	Asche
5.	Heise II	30.	Probst II	55.	Grüne
6.	Dauer	31.	Schmidt I	56.	Schumacher I
7.	Schmidt II	32.	Schoppe	57.	Heise IV
8.	Schünemann 1	33.	Diekmann I	58.	Schmidt V
9.	Wöhning	34.	Schmidt III	59.	Esser
10.	Niemeyer	35.	Weber	60.	Peinecke
11.	Lamse I	36.	Dormann	61.	Hilmer II
12.	Probst I	37.	Schäfer	62.	Timmermann II
13.	Siebrecht	38.	Verzagt	63.	Winzmann
14.	Winnefeld	39.	Specht	64.	Schaumann II
15.	Jakob	40.	Schmidt IV	65.	Bremer
16.	Wegener I	41.	Bock	66.	Diekmann IV
17.	Lanze	42.	Schaumann I	67.	Dormann "
18.	Hesse	43.	Spormann	68.	Klages "
19.	Wegener II	44.	Teives	69.	Dauer "
20.	Olms	45.	Kühne		
21.	Diekmann II	46.	Schünemann II		
22.	Wegener III	47.	Schwake		
23.	Kronberg	48.	Hartmann		
24.	Czepluch	49.	Schumacher II		
25.	Heise III	50.	Diekmann III		

The era of joint decision-making by blue-collar and white-collar workers began in the Weimar Republic in 1920, when the Works Council Constitution Act came into force. Accordingly, companies with more than twenty employees had to elect a works council. The Symrise works council archive contains the first documents from 1923. The lists of Haarmann & Reimer workers and employees entitled to vote provide a good overview of the 90-strong workforce at the plant at the time.

New Beginnings …

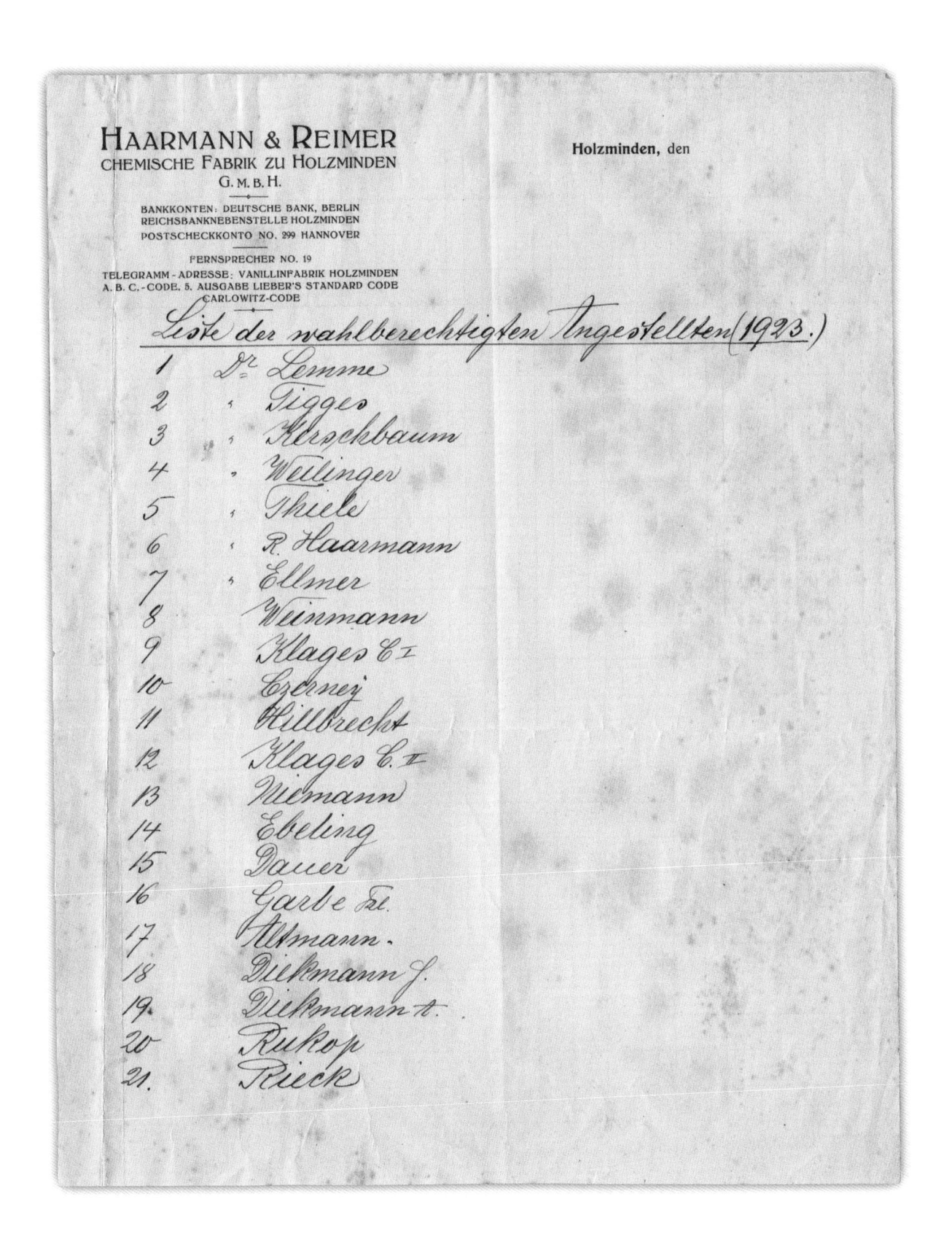

HAARMANN & REIMER
CHEMISCHE FABRIK ZU HOLZMINDEN
G. M. B. H.

Holzminden, den

BANKKONTEN: DEUTSCHE BANK, BERLIN
REICHSBANKNEBENSTELLE HOLZMINDEN
POSTSCHECKKONTO NO. 299 HANNOVER
FERNSPRECHER NO. 19
TELEGRAMM-ADRESSE: VANILLINFABRIK HOLZMINDEN
A. B. C.-CODE, 5. AUSGABE LIEBER'S STANDARD CODE
CARLOWITZ-CODE

<u>Liste der wahlberechtigten Angestellten (1923.)</u>

1. Dr. Lemme
2. „ Tigges
3. „ Kirschbaum
4. „ Wellinger
5. „ Thiele
6. „ R. Haarmann
7. „ Ellmer
8. Weinmann
9. Klages C. I
10. Czerney
11. Hillbrecht
12. Klages C. II
13. Niemann
14. Ebeling
15. Dauer
16. Garbe H.
17. Altmann
18. Dickmann J.
19. Dickmann A.
20. Rukop
21. Rieck

the emerging liberal state also offered hopeful prospects for growth. This was evidenced by the number of new companies registered, which reached a record high in 1919. Carl Wilhelm Gerberding recognised the spirit of the times and acted accordingly.

1924 – 50 years Haarmann & Reimer

The 50th anniversary of Haarmann & Reimer in 1924 coincided with a phase of stabilisation in the economy as a whole. There is no mention of crises in the anniversary brochure: The history of the company was presented, and an overview of the current products and photographs of the factory premises and production were shown. The text also mentioned that over the past twenty years, Haarmann & Reimer had set itself the task of "researching the fragrances of our sweet-smelling garden flowers. [...] In order to research this, experimental fields first had to be created". In addition to a lavender plantation on the Burgberg near Bevern, mignonette and lupine plantations were also planted in Allersheimer Kirchweg in Holzminden. It went on to say that the costly scientific research had proven to be very difficult: *"Some of these fragrances are only present in extremely small quantities, but are, nevertheless, indispensable if a fragrance identical to the floral scent is to be created. Therefore, very subtle methods of investigation had to be*

Title page and images from the brochure marking the 50th anniversary of Haarmann & Reimer in 1924

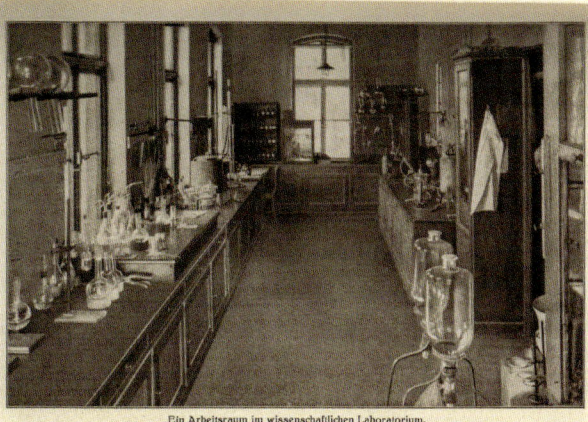

developed [...] Dr. M. Kerschbaum deserves special credit for this extremely difficult chemical work." It went on to say that it was regrettable "*that the patent courts and the processing by the courts do not afford protection for the [...] inventions, and that, therefore, this extraordinarily interesting scientific work cannot be published.*"
The photos in the anniversary brochure shows an impressive factory site that stretched between the streets An den Teichen and Fabrikstrasse (later Rumohrtalstrasse). Since the turn of the century, the company had not only erected its own factory buildings, but also bought up neighbouring businesses and installed its own production facilities in the buildings.

1927 – More than 100 employees at Haarmann & Reimer

Haarmann & Reimer now called itself a producer of "speciality products for the manufacture of sugar confectionery, liqueurs, baked goods and non-alcoholic beverages". In the mid-1920s, the company was able to re-establish its international business relations. In 1927, the company had more than 100 employees.
To celebrate the 80th birthday of its founder on 24 May 1927, the entire workforce travelled to Höxter on a chartered train.

The Haarmann & Reimer management team in 1927 with Wilhelm Haarmann Jr. (left), and Max Kerschbaum (second from left)

1919 – 1945

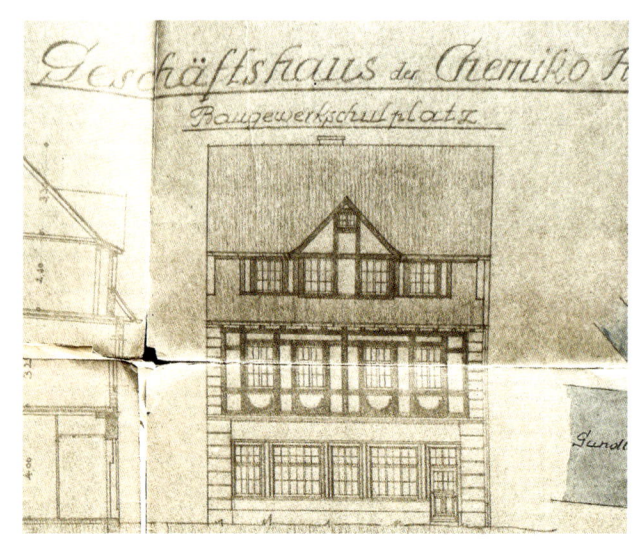

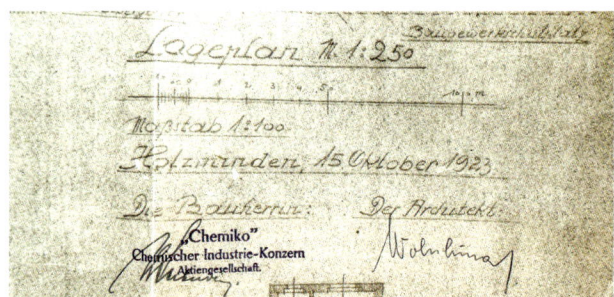

During the inflation period, Carl-Wilhelm Gerberding founded the chemical company Chemiko, which, in addition to Dragoco, also incorporated several older chemical companies. The first commercial building of Chemiko was to be built in Fürstenberger Strasse. The plan shown above and dated October 1923 was found in the Holzminden town archives. However, the building had to be sold again in 1924. In 1928, Central Drugstore Somborn opened in this building.

1926 – Dragoco's first production facilities

Until 1925, Dragoco was, in principle, a small laboratory business, which had survived the period of inflation reasonably well. In 1926, an extension behind Gerberding's home at Bahnhofstrasse 6 was added to create the company's first production facilities - the initial step to turning Dragoco into an industrial company.

1928 – Dragoco PLC

In 1923, C.W. Gerberding had already converted his company into a public limited company and manoeuvred it through the period of inflation and the economy crisis with various financial transactions. However, until then, Dragoco PLC was a modest company. The register of the German Limited Companies of 1928 listed it as follows:

"Dragoco Aktiengesellschaft ätherische Öle und künstliche Riechstoffe in Holzminden, purpose: manufacture of products of the chemical industry and trade in such products; acquisition of related companies or companies serving the purposes of the company and participation in such companies. Company name (until 1925) Chemiko, Chemischer Industriekonzern, Aktiengesellschaft Hannover, dividends 1923 to 1927 0% in each case".

Just as Wilhelm Haarmann had registered international patents very early and presented his vanillin at the World Exhibition in the USA, C.W. Gerberding and August Bellmer were acting with great foresight, as the acquisition of companies was later to become a major growth factor.

The Vanillin Convention in the 1920s

In the mid-1920s, the annual demand for vanillin in Europe was around 70,000 kg. While Haarmann & Reimer had set up the first cartel on their own initiative in the 19th century due to increasing competition, the situation was now completely different. A large-scale chemical industry had emerged and it also had its sights set

New Beginnings ...

Haarmann & Reimer
chemische Fabrik zu Holzminden
G. m. b. H.

Holzminden, den 13. November 1928.

An die J. G. Farbenindustrie A.-G.,
Verkaufsgemeinschaft Chemikalien,
Abteilung Z III,
Frankfurt/M., Gutleutstr. 31,

und J. G. Farbenindustrie A.-G.
Agfa - Riechstoffe,
Berlin SO 36, Lohmühlenstr. 65.

Vanillin.

Nach Mitteilung der Chemischen Werke Grenzach A.-G. haben Sie im Monat Oktober wieder 2386,660 Kilo Vanillin geliefert. Sie haben damit Ihre Quote wiederum um ein Erhebliches überschritten.

Sie haben geliefert im

			an die Konvention:
II. Quartal 1928:	Verkäufe	2008,355 kg,	1500 kg,
III. " " :	"	3892,120 kg	---
Oktober 1928:	"	2386,660 kg	---
		8287,135 kg	1500 kg.

Dagegen beträgt Ihre Berechtigung:

II. Quartal 1928:	Verkäufe	1250,000 kg	1500 kg,
III. " " :	"	1250,000 kg	1500 kg
Oktober 1928:	"	416,670 kg	500 kg
		2916,670 kg	3500 kg.

Sie haben also zuviel verkauft: 5370,465 kg
und zu wenig an die Konvention geliefert: 2000,000 kg.

Ihre Jahresberechtigung haben Sie damit schon bis zum 1. November um 1537,135 kg überschritten.

Wir müssen auch im Namen der übrigen Konventionsmitglieder unserer Verwunderung Ausdruck geben, daß Sie sich über den von Ihnen geschlossenen Vertrag in so auffälliger Weise hinwegsetzen, und bitten Sie um Ihre Stellungnahme, in welcher Weise Sie die durch Ihr Vorgehen verursachte

---

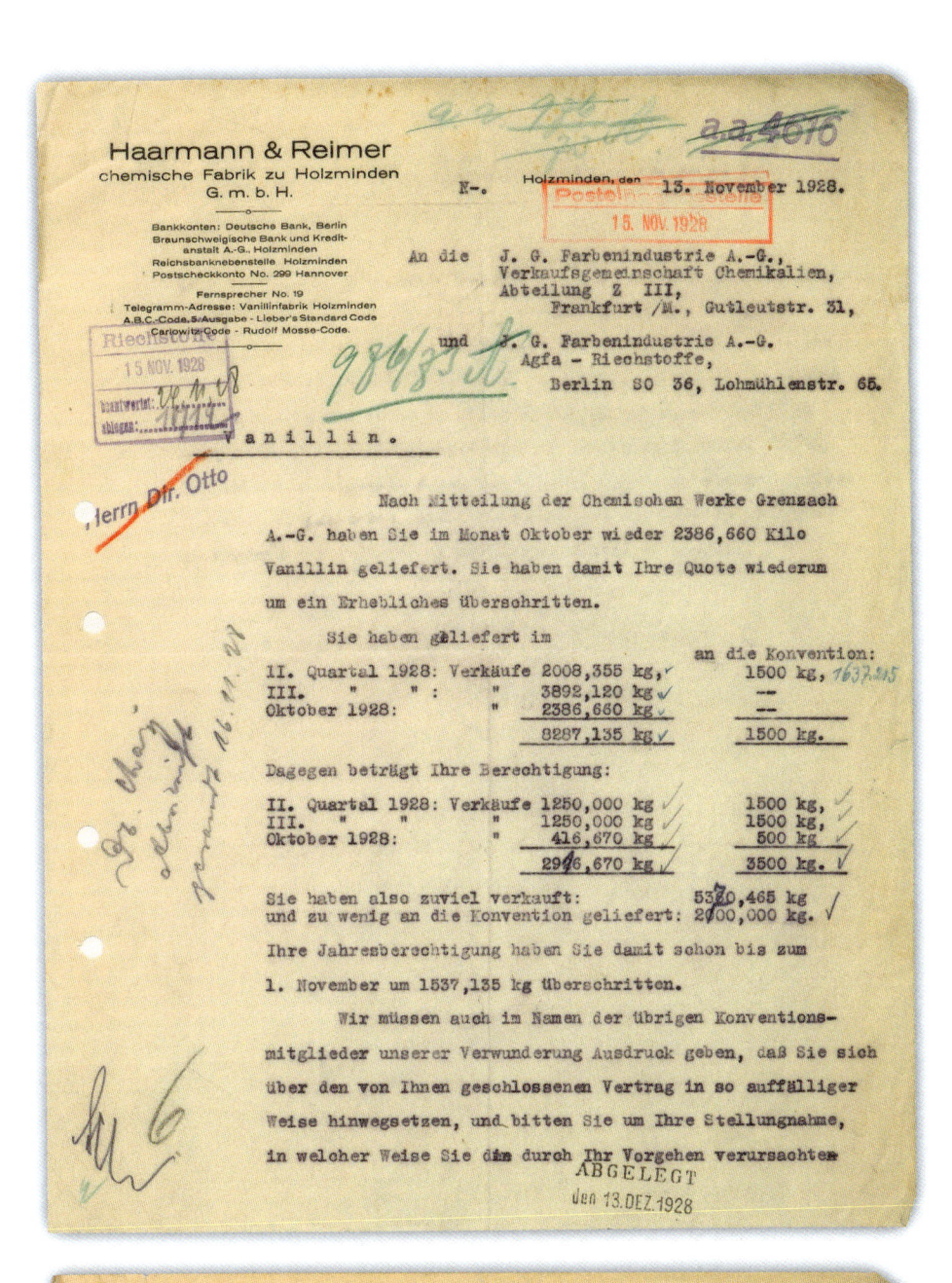

Haarmann & Reimer G.m.b.H. Blatt: 2 Holzminden, den 13.11.28.
chemische Fabrik zu Holzminden
J. G. Farbenindustrie A.-G., Frankfurt,
und Firma Agfa-Riechstoffe, Berlin SO 36.

ganz erhebliche Schädigung der übrigen Vertragspartner gutzumachen gedenken.

Sie haben Ihre steigenden Verkäufe nur dadurch bewirken können, daß Sie die Konventionsmitglieder im Auslande vielfach unterboten haben. Wir selbst haben in mehreren Fällen auf Ihre billigeren Angebote hin bestehende Abschlüsse im Preise herabsetzen müssen. Das sollte aber gerade durch den Vertrag vermieden werden, nachdem Sie sich verpflichtet haben, Ihre Verkäufe auf 5000 kg im Jahre zu beschränken und 6000 kg an die Konvention zu liefern.

Hochachtungsvoll
Haarmann & Reimer
chemische Fabrik zu Holzminden G.m.b.H.

This letter from Haarmann & Reimer to "I. G. Farbenindustrie A.-G. Agfa-Riechstoffe" (IG Dye Factory A.-G. Agfa Fragrances) provides an insight into the intentions of the Vanillin Convention and the difficulties resulting from the basic competitive situation of the partners.

on the fragrance market. Agfa (Public Limited Company for Aniline Production), part of I.G. Farben (Dye Industry Syndicate), planned to produce large quantities of vanillin from the readily available guaiacol. In this context, I.G. Farben founded the Vanillin Convention, which Haarmann & Reimer, as the largest vanillin manufacturer to date, had to join for better or worse. Boehringer Mannheim, Grenzach and Hoffmann-la-Roche also joined.

There were no holds barred within this partnership. In her book, *A History With Flavour – The Nature Of Synthetic Aroma Materials In The 20th Century Using Vanillin As An Example*, Paulina S. Gennermann quotes an internal discussion from 1928 using the minutes which the author had found in the historical archives of the company Roche. Under the heading 'Disagreement in the Vanillin Convention' it noted for example that a representative of I.G. Farben demanded that *"Holminden be shut down"*, to which Dr. Jacoby from the chemical factory in Griesheim countered: *"H&R cannot be stopped. They will continue to produce as long as they still have the eugenol process."*

Dr. Boehring is then quoted: *"Incidentally, H&R is not as insignificant as it is being portrayed. 2/3 of their sales go abroad."* Quotes by Otto from I.G. Farben also show *"the suggestion not to supply H&R is not acceptable for Agfa. The conglomerate has, however, decided in the general interest to bring a further sacrifice. Agfa would settle for 32% of an international quota. This would, however, be the very minimum."*

The background of this discussion was, among other topics, the production network and the delivery chains which I.G. Farben wanted to control. For while their companies were employing the guaiacol process, Haarmann and Reimer continued to use the time-tested and also higher-quality eugenol process. As the clove oil which was necessary for this process did not come from I.G. Farben but was purchased from a Hamburg company which was not part of the conglomerate, I.G. Farben wanted to, if not completely eliminate Haarmann & Reimer, at least control it as much as possible and prevent it from increasing production. There were also international cartels alongside this German-Swiss convention in which the German companies participated in various constellations.

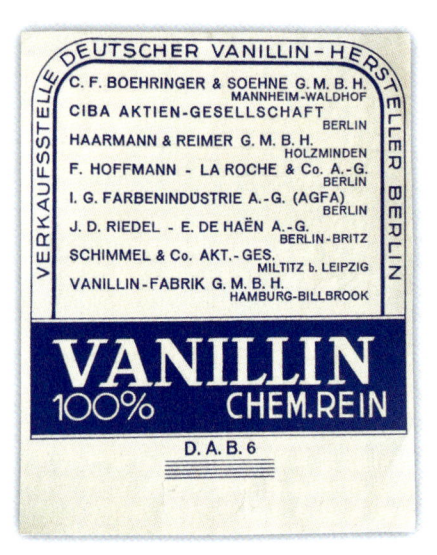

In the 1920s, the Vanillin Convention was geared towards the international market. The label shown above is from a later period and documents the fact that the National Socialist rulers nationalised the Vanillin Convention and transformed it into a "sales office for German vanillin manufacturers".

Advertisement for Dragoco A.G. in a trade journal

Fabrikansicht unseres Werkes in Holzminden a. W.

1929 – Dragoco moves to Sollingstrasse

In 1929, Dragoco took over an old iron foundry in Sollingstrasse and set up production and administration there. The company, hereby, moved onto the current company premises of Symrise Solling site in Wiesenweg. The new production hall enabled Dragoco, now with 30 employees, to also begin producing flavours and food aromas.

Some of the photos taken in the early days of Dragoco, showing the administrative and production facilities, cannot entirely conceal the fact that the company has moved into the production hall of an old iron foundry.

1919 – 1945

The Schimmel & Co factory in Miltitz near Leipzig

The reports by Schimmel & Co emphasised the company's aspiration of scientific leadership in the field of essential oils and fragrances.

Wilhelm Haarmann

1929 – 100 years Schimmel & Co

Although Haarmann & Reimer had an important technical reputation and business was also developing well at the end of the 1920s, the Holzminden fragrance and flavouring industry, with a total of less than 150 employees, could be described as modest compared to the large chemical industry: The I.G. Farben (Dye Industry Syndicate) companies (with the main players Bayer, BASF and Hoechst) had a total of almost 100,000 employees in 1929. The only fragrance company to achieve larger economic significance at that time was Schimmel & Co A.G. in Miltitz near Leipzig. It had resulted from a merger, in 1927, between Schimmel, founded in 1829, and the Leipzig company E. Sachsse & Co.

Around 1900, Schimmel had erected a highly modern industrial complex in Miltitz near Leipzig with workers' houses and a neighbourhood with mansions for the chemists and more senior employees. On 1 September 1929, more than 1,000 guests came to celebrate the 100th anniversary of this traditional company. One of the letters of congratulations which was read out was from the Saxony Ministry of Economics and declared: *"Your company has established its leading position in the economy and its worldwide reputation in the field of the extraction of volatile oils from the plant world and the production of essential oils and fragrances in a century of determined and restless work in the Leipzig branch. Its global connections are expressed not only in the fact that the company obtains its raw materials from all over the world, but also exports its products to all the world's recognised countries."* This was coupled with the wish that the company may continue to succeed in *"fully maintaining its position as a leading company in its economic sector on the world market in the future."*

1931– Death of Wilhelm Haarmann

Wilhelm Haarmann died in 1931. He was buried in a grave of honour in Höxter cemetery. Dr. A. Elmer, Geneva, wrote in his obituary in the professional journal Riechstoff Industrie (Fragrance Industry): *"If there is one place where this richly blessed life can be remembered in a particularly grateful way, then it is in these pages which bear the name of the industry in which Wilhelm Haarmann played a leading role in its founding and promotion."* Elmer wrote about the founding of Haarmann's Vanillin Factory: *"The commencement of this production must be regarded as an economic act of the first order. [...] The concept of fragrance chemistry as a distinct branch of research as we know it today did not exist at that time, let alone an industry of artificial fragrances. [...] The beginnings of an essential oil industry can be found as early as the first half of the 19th century in the ventures of some Saxon companies (Schimmel, Heine, Sachsse, Hänsel etc.). However, it was not until 1884 that Otto Wallach had begun his ground-breaking work on essential oils and their components which was to lead this industry in the field of empiricism on a scientific basis for development. Haarmann worked together with Tiemann, the great master, to whose systematic research the essential oil industry owes so much, and who was ten years ahead in the practical evaluation of the scientific work in the newly developing field.*

New Beginnings ...

Haarmann & Reimer's lavender fields, colour photograph from the 1930s.

[...] *The annual worldwide consumption of vanillin is estimated to be 500,000 kg, which is supplied by approximately 20 large companies. This highlights just how much of a factor Wilhelm Haarmann's first establishment has become in the global economy."*
Wilhelm Haarmann was managing director of the company until his death at the age of 83. His sons Wilhelm and Reinhold then took over the management of Haarmann & Reimer.

Lavender fields on the Burgberg
The professional journal *Riechstoff-Industrie* (Fragrance Industry) reported on the lavender fields of Haarmann & Reimer on the Burgberg near Bevern. It states: *"It is quite obvious that this lavender extract which has been won in Germany cannot make much of an impression on the general requirements."*
Nevertheless, Haarmann & Reimer was able to use the lavender fields later to impress those in power: A report dated 1943 to District Leader Laue documents a reference to the lavender fields on the Burgberg: *"The lavender field was harvested for the first time last year and then again this year as part of the medicinal plant collection for the HJ (Hitler Youth) and the yield was allocated to the intended purposes via the responsible authorities."*

Max Kerschbaum in the lavender field at Burgberg near Bevern

Timber saccharification

In 1936, the "economically important" third largest chemical company in Holzminden, Braunschweigische Holzverzuckerungs KG W. Grotrian-Steinweg (Brunswick Timber Saccharification Company), was established using state subsidies. It was taken over by Holzverzuckerungsgesellschaft mbH (Timber Saccharification Company) in 1938. Large percolators and distillation plants were installed on the site of the former Bärtling vinegar factory to produce sugar from the sawdust from the town's numerous wood-processing industries. Alcohol was extracted from this after fermentation and distillation. During the war years, nutrients and raw spirits were produced. After the Second World War, success was achieved in the production of fine spirits for liqueurs and potable spirits. Around 1950, production was up to 400,000 litres per month and 230 people were employed there. However, production had to be discontinued by the end of the 1950s. Paper was produced at the plant until the mid-1980s. The site was later taken over by Haarmann & Reimer and the buildings demolished.

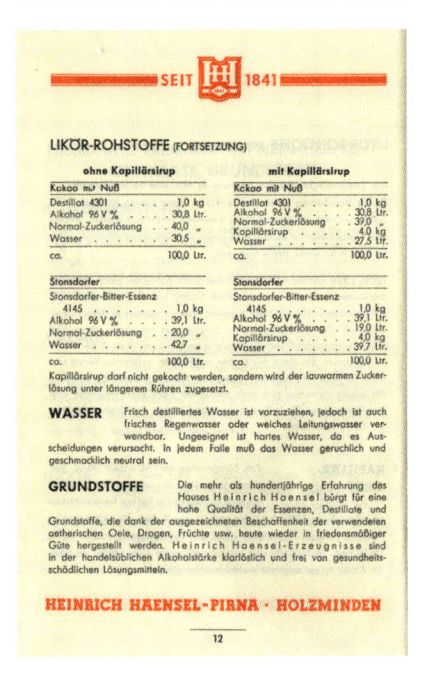

Page from a Haensel price list; the company specialised in essences for the beverage industry.

1933 – Upswing in the food industry

After power was handed over to the National Socialists in 1933, the food industry first enjoyed an upswing. Vanillin which was produced in Germany was preferred in the manufacture of food as a replacement for the missing imports which had resulted from Hitler's efforts to make Germany self-sufficient. It was mainly Dr. Oetker which needed vanillin to flavour custard powder for the Army. Despite increasing shortages, vanillin was comparatively easy to produce and proved to be a favourite custard flavour.

1934 – 60th Anniversary Haarmann & Reimer

The text of the brochure marking the 60th anniversary of Haarmann & Reimer is partly taken word for word from the publication marking the 50th anniversary. The following information was added: "*Successful work was also carried out in the company's scientific laboratory in the highly interesting and difficult field of animalic scents. [...] Lacon 'Ambretttolid' ($C_{16}H_{28}O_2$) was the practical result of this work and does, in fact, contain vegetal musk scent, a highly valuable scent in perfumery, in the highest purity and concentration.*"

Significant progress has also been made in the field of alkali resistance of the most important natural and artificial fragrances: "*When using these soap perfumes, the perfumer can, therefore, be assured that neither the composition of the soap will be damaged by the perfume (e.g. becomes rancid, discoloured) nor will the alkali of the soap cause decomposition or loss of the soap fragrance.*"

The success of the business was also reflected in the fact that Haarmann & Reimer invested in Noelle & von Campe Glassworks in Boffzen in the "*interest of supporting local industry*". This was clearly a means of support because the existence of the company was at risk.

1935 – Dragoco purchased the company Heinrich Haensel

In 1935, C.W. Gerberding realised its corporate objective of "acquiring or investing in similar companies" with the successful acquisition of Heinrich Haensel: Founded in Pirna in 1841, the company was an established supplier of essential oils and beverage flavourings, which enabled Dragoco to significantly expand its product range.

Haensel was one of the first companies of the essence industry to produce essential oils which were free from terpene and sesquiterpene and had made a name for itself, in particular, in researching and identifying the ingredients of essential oils. By purchasing Haensel, Dragoco also acquired expertise in the field of research which certainly benefitted the expansion of their own research department, which, until then, had been rather modest.

At the time the company was purchased, the company's products were being sold worldwide. The 1941 catalogue for the 100th anniversary of Haensel contained

New Beginnings ...

numerous essences, basic ingredients and compound formulas for all types of liqueurs, spirits and lemonades.

As the international market had more or less collapsed in the 1930s and, in particular, during the war, the domestic market was initially the main customer for the artificial beverage flavourings as they replaced numerous imported products. Dragoco had 57 employees in 1935.

1937 – Dragoco expanded

Dragoco was converted into a limited partnership: Dragoco, Spezialfabrik konzentrierter Riech- und Aromastoffe, Gerberding & Co., Holzminden (Dragoco, Special Factory for Concentrated Fragrances and Flavourings, Gerberding & Co., Holzminden). With 33 employees and 64 workers, Dragoco had close to 40 per cent more employees than two years previously and generated a turnover of 2.1 million Reichsmarks.

Dragoco price list from 1940

Photos from the 1930s and 1940s at Dragoco

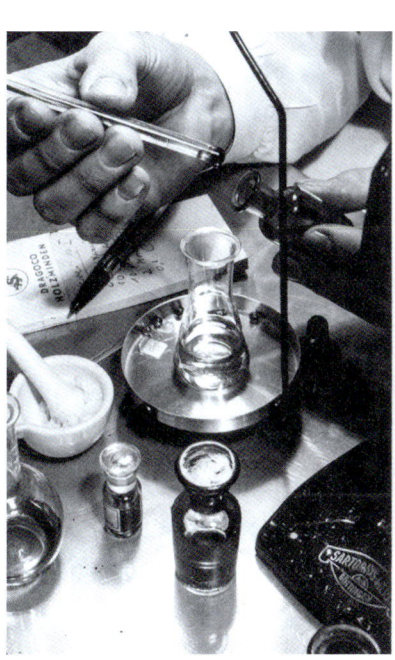

1919 – 1945

Dragoco in the 1940s. The large number of working women suggests that the photos were taken during the war; only a few men were exempt from military service.

New Beginnings ...

1937 – More holidays for the 'followers'

A four-page, lavishly designed History Of The Company by Haarmann & Reimer dates from February 1937. Clearly in keeping with the National Socialist zeitgeist, it focuses on the achievements for the 'followers' comprising 50 blue collar and 30 white collar workers. In addition to the construction of houses and flats, it emphasises that *"in July 1934 [...] annual leave for workers was extended to 18 working days"*. From 1935, weekly instead of hourly wages were introduced and in *"May 1935, the company introduced the payment of 3 days sick leave by the company health insurance fund for sick workers."* In addition, in 1934, 1935 and 1936, a total of 21 workers and employees were granted *"free 8-day holiday trips with payment of an allowance."* All participants had decided in favour of a cruise to Norway. *"The intention for 1937 is to reduce the number of camaraderie and company evenings [...] and instead increase the number of free holiday trips."*

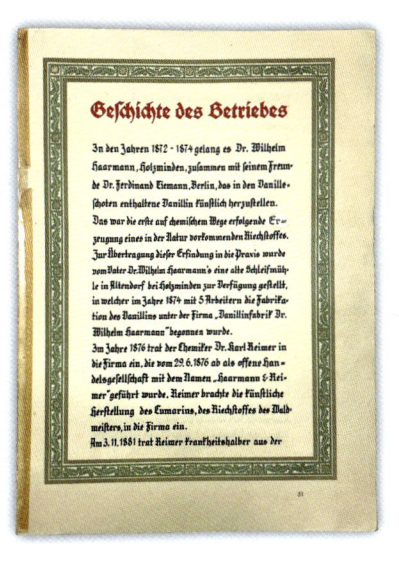

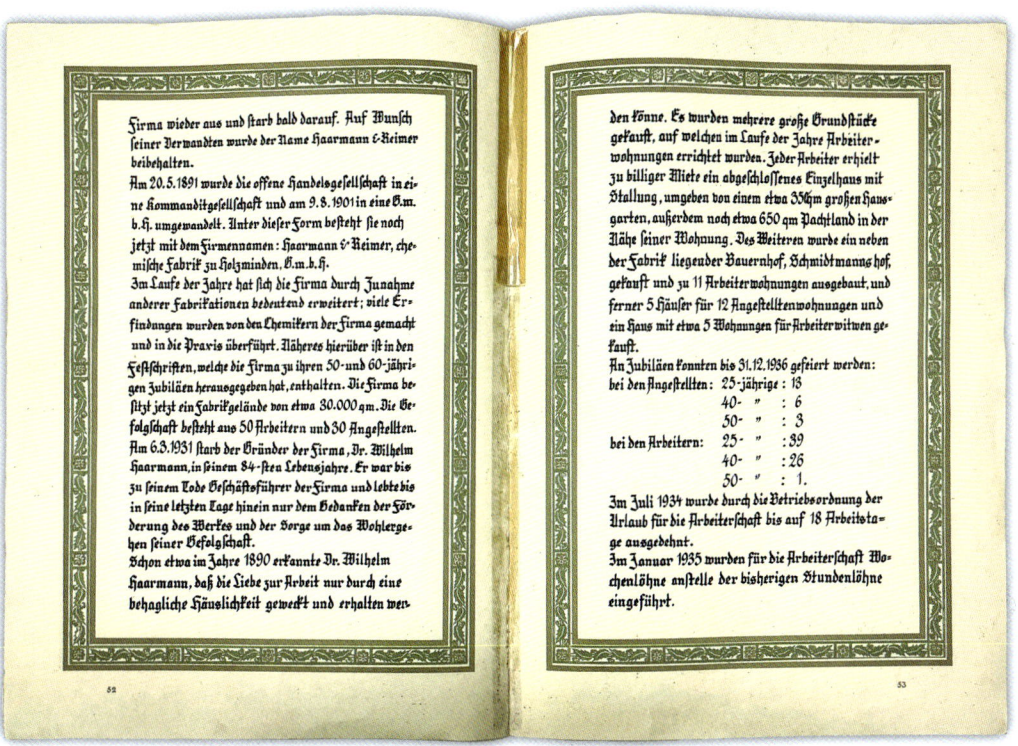

It can be assumed that the *"sea voyages to Norway"* were *"strength through joy"* trips. This mass organisation, founded by the National Socialists, extended the totalitarian hold of the Nazi regime to travel and holidays. On the one hand, it enabled ordinary working-class families to take holiday trips for the first time. On the other hand, the real aim was to toughen up the *"Aryan"* worker for a growing economy and ultimately to turn the Germans into a nation fit for war.

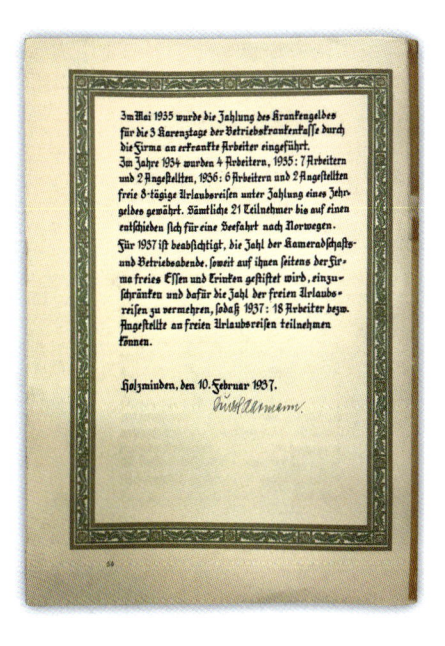

Photographs of Haarmann & Reimer production from the 1920s. The majority of these machines were only modernised in the 1950s.

New Beginnings ...

1939 – Vanillin as a replacement for cocoa

The well-researched publication by Paulina S. Gemmermann notes that the demand for vanillin grew significantly at the end of the 1930s. The efforts of the National Socialist rulers to become self-sufficient meant that many imported goods, including cocoa, became scarce and, as such, the consumption of flavoured foods increased.

The Bielefeld company Dr. Oetker required approximately one third of the vanillin production of the Vanillin Convention: In the first half of 1938, the company was supplied with 18,550 kg vanillin from Boehringer Mannheim, Agfa, Hoffmann-la-Roche Berlin and Haarmann & Reimer. In 1939, it rose to more than 33 tonnes vanillin and approximately 6 tonnes ethyl vanillin. A further increase of around 30% was estimated for 1940. After this enormous increase in production, the food manufacturers could hardly envisage that vanillin would become scarce but that was soon to change.

After the international cartels had been dissolved at the beginning of the Second World War, the structure of the Vanillin Convention was continued by the participating German companies Boehringer Mannheim, Hoffmann-la-Roche Berlin, Agfa, Riedel-de Haën, Schimmel, Haarmann & Reimer and Vanillin-Fabrik Hamburg under the name German Vanillin Convention.

Curious find in the archives: cleaning a boiler in 1934

Dr. F. Alexander Bene
Dr. L. Summerer
Ruf: 65845 Draht: Syndik D'df.
Commerz- und Privatbank A.-G.
Düsseldorf
Postscheck 12755 Essen

Düsseldorf, den
Paulusstr. 1

31. März 1938.

An die Firmen

C.F. Boehringer & Soehne GmbH.,	Mannheim-Waldhof
Haarmann & Reimer GmbH.,	Holzminden
F. Hoffmann-La Roche & Co. AG.,	Basel
F. Hoffmann-La Roche & Co. AG.,	Berlin-Charlottenburg
Berlin, Chemische Fabrik,	Berlin-Britz
JD. Riedel-E.de Haen AG.,	Miltitz b/Leipzig
Schimmel & Co. AG.,	
IG Farbenindustrie Aktien-	
gesellschaft, Agfa Riechstoffe,	Berlin SO 36
Vanillin-Fabrik GmbH.,	Hamburg
Verkaufsstelle Deutscher Vanillin-	
Hersteller, Berlin,	Berlin W 50.

Vanillin/ Aethylvanillin.

Im Monat F e b r u a r 1938 lieferten:

	Vanillin	Aethylvanillin
Agfa	1 252 kg 942 g	123 kg 000 g
Roche Berlin	1 267 kg 000 g	50 kg 000 g
Holzminden	1 816 kg 163 g	621 kg 375 g
Waldhof	2 298 kg 807 g	99 kg 000 g
Schimmel	1 498 kg 912 g	130 kg 825 g
Britz/Hamburg	1 281 kg 659 g	140 kg 110 g
Roche Basel	531 kg 250 g	40 kg 500 g
	9 946 kg 733 g	1 204 kg 810 g

Hochachtungsvoll

While the company sold a total of 169,929.625 kg of vanillin in 1940, the quantity fell to just under 40 tonnes in 1942. Vanillin became a scarce commodity, with the result that, in 1943, flavouring with vanillin and ethyl vanillin was only permitted for foodstuffs subject to ration cards (e.g. custard powder) and for military supplies. Although the Vanillin Convention was unsuccessful in achieving official recognition of vanillin as *"essential to the war effort"* at both the Reich Ministry of Economics and of Food, it seemed, as Gennermann surmises, that both substances had special standing.

1940 – Vanillin from sulphite liquor
A letter dated 29 July 1940 (Symrise archive) sheds an interesting light on vanillin production of that time. In it, the companies of I.G. Farben (Dye Industry Syndicate) inform Riedel-de Haën, Schimmel & Co and Haarmann & Reimer: *"The undersigned companies hereby inform their Convention friends that they have decided to combine their processes and patent rights based on lengthy individual research concerning the production of crude vanillin from sulphite liquors and to continue the evaluation of this production method by founding a company with a production facility on the premises of the company C. F. Boehringer & Soehne G.m.b.H. in the near future."* In this letter, the other companies are offered the opportunity to purchase the raw vanillin produced in this way and use it to produce pure vanillin in their own plants. The documents show that the Haarmann & Reimer representatives were extremely surprised by this proposal, to say the least. The archives contain minutes of a meeting with Dr. Scholz of Schimmel & Co, in which it says: *"Dr. Scholz also stated quite frankly that his company was of the opinion that the proposal of the three*

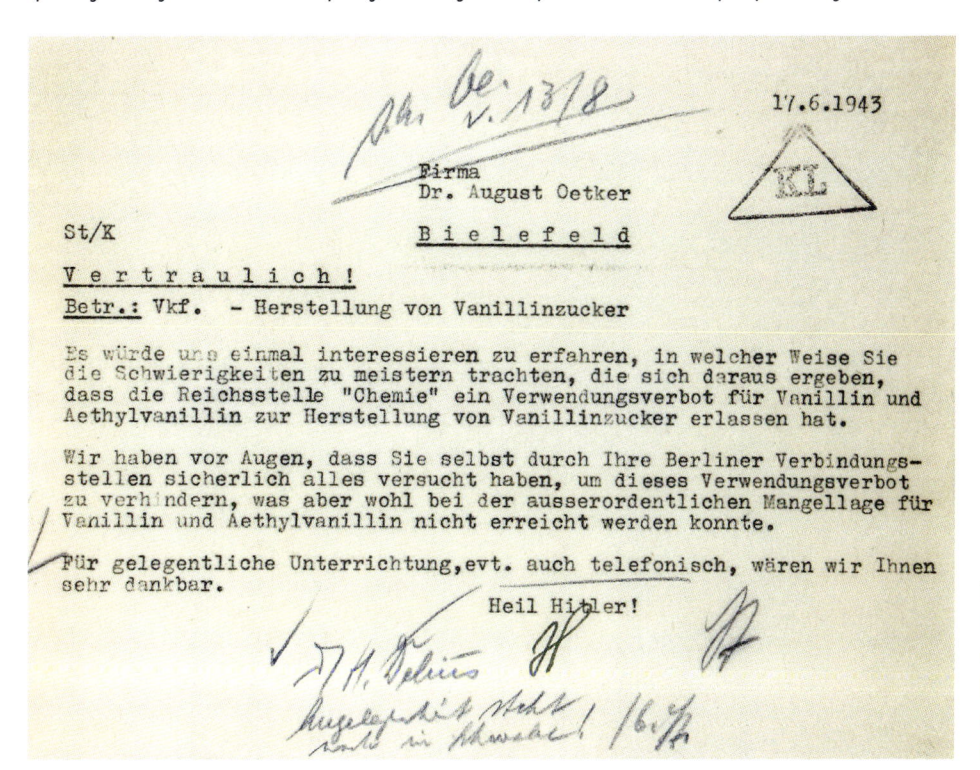

This confidential letter from Haarmann & Reimer to the Oetker company in Bielefeld highlights the shortages that existed during the Second World War.

1919 – 1945

In wartime, images of tropical fruit must have had a special appeal. With this 1940s advert, Haarmann & Reimer implied that people did not have to go without the taste of these fruits thanks to artificial flavourings.

Trade fair in Milan: International business was extremely limited due to the policies of the National Socialists and the War. Participating in a trade fair in Mussolini's Italy was one of the few international activities of Haarmann & Reimer during this period.

New Beginnings ...

syndicate companies would have to be accepted, for better or for worse." In view of the monopolised production of vanillin, however, there was a risk.

In another set of minutes of a conversation with Mr. Fritzsching from the Boehringer company, there is an interesting detail that indicates that, in 1940, the German companies were already looking ahead to the time after the war: *"In the course of the conversation, Fritzsching mentioned, among other things, that an agreement with Monsanto Canada regarding the reservation of sales territories for one group or another could certainly be expected later."*

Coffarom fails to establish itself

Haarmann & Reimer launched an ersatz coffee onto the market under the name Coffarom (*"patented in all recognised countries"*) in the 1930s. An advertising leaflet states: *"For the first time, we have succeeded together with fellow researchers in unravelling this complicated composition [of the coffee aroma], characterising the individual components and, finally, in reconstructing the mixture synthetically."* Additional advantages are emphasized: *"Significant reduction in costs / simplified processing / no loss of valuable volatile aroma constituents during storage"*. However, both during and after the Second World War, Coffarom was unable to assert itself against both malt and chicory coffee which had been tried and tested in the First World War.

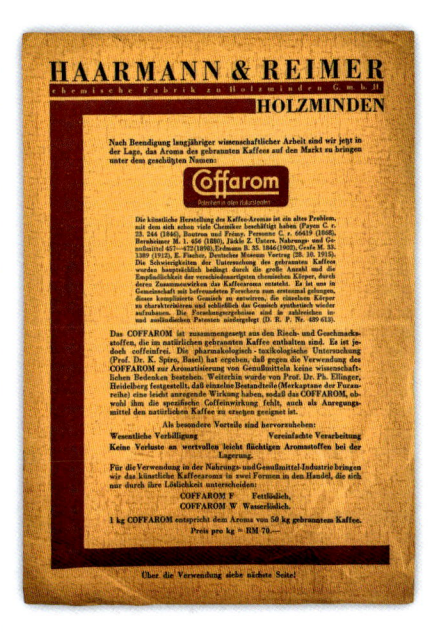

Information sheet on Coffarom from the 1940s

Foreign participation became 'hostile participation'

As mentioned above, Haarmann & Reimer had already established business relations with the French company de Laire shortly after it was founded when both companies had taken over shares from each other. While the German shareholding in de Laire was expropriated after the First World War, de Laire retained its shares in Haarmann & Reimer. At the beginning of the Second World War, the Haarmann and Tiemann group of heirs each held a 27.5% stake in Haarmann & Reimer, while the French group held a 45% stake.

This constellation led to various problems in the Second World War because Edgar de Laire was not only one of the three members of the supervisory board, he was also French.

According to the Ordinance on the Treatment of Enemy Assets of 15 January 1940, Haarmann & Reimer had to report the enemy shares. No payments could be made to the enemy, nor could the enemy's assets be disposed of.

When Edgar de Laire died in 1941 followed by Kuno Tiemann in 1943, the supervisory board was rendered incapable of operating and the lawyer G. Becker was appointed administrator of the 'enemy assets'. A report to the British military administration dated 4 December 1945 states: *"At the shareholders' meeting on 26 January 1944, the following gentlemen were elected as members of the company's supervisory board: Mr. Becker, lawyer and notary, Hannover / Dr. Marheine, lawyer*

Anmeldung feindlichen Vermögens

Anmeldebogen D

Bezeichnung des Unternehmens: Haarmann & Reimer, chemische Fabrik zu Holzminden G.m.b.H.

in Holzminden   Fernsprechanschluss: 619

Name und Anschriften der Anmeldenden (Geschäftsführers – zur Geschäftsführung berufenen Gesellschafter)

       Haarmann, Reinhold, Dr.phil., Holzminden
       Axt, Wilhelm, Holzminden

I. Angaben betreffend das Unternehmen

1. Gegenstand des Unternehmens Herstellung von synthetischen Riech- und Würzstoffen

Namen und Anschriften	Staatsangehörigkeit d.Gesellsch.	Stammkapital	Nennbetrag des Anteils
Dr.W.Haarmann's Erben, Holzminden	Deutschland	449 800	123 700
Prof.Dr.F.Tiemann's Erben, Berlin SW 15	"		123 700
Edgar de Laire, Paris, 228 rue de l'Université	Frankreich		123 700
A.Max' Erben, Neuilly s/Seine 3 Boul.Richard Wallace	Frankreich		31 500
Frau H. Marqueste, Versailles, 2 Rue Maurepas	"		23 600
Jacques Robert, Brüssel, 87 rue Washington	Belgien		23 600

Wert d.Anteils 400% ?   Schlußsumme der letzten Bilanz 31.12.1938 2134579.10

Feindliche Beteiligte am 31.12.39   *Wert des Anteils 400% ?*

	Staatsangehörigkt	Nennbetrag des Anteils
Edgar de Laire, Paris 228 rue de l'Université	Frankreich	123700.–
A.Max' Erben, Neuilly s/Seine 3 Boul.Richard Wallace	"	31500.–
Frau H.Marqueste, Versailles, 2 rue Maurepas	"	23600.–

am 1.7.38 ebenso wie am 31.12.39

Haarmann & Reimer
chemische Fabrik zu Holzminden G.m.b.H.

H, 29.3.40.

"*Registration of hostile assets*" by Haarmann & Reimer in March 1940

and notary, Brunswick / Mr. Diesener, lawyer and notary, Holzminden / The remaining member of the Supervisory Board after the deaths of Mr. de Laire and Mr. Tiemann, Dr. W. Haarmann, Holzminden, was not re-elected due to reservations expressed by the Reich Commissioner for the Handling of Enemy Assets about electing a managing director as a member of the supervisory board [...]."

It also states that, in 1943, the companies Dr. Oetker and Riedel-de Haën had approached the German shareholders independently of one another to buy up the hostile shares. "*As these companies informed us, they had also approached several foreign shareholders in this regard, but with what result, we are not aware. The negotiations with the German shareholders were fruitless.*"

In her book, Paulina S. Gennermann quotes from a letter to this effect from Dr. Oetker, in which the company also pointed out "*that these shares were not only 'enemy assets', but in part Jewish capital or capital subject to Jewish influence, which would certainly have to be transferred into Aryan hands one day*".

1940 – Aryanisation of Dutch companies by Haarmann & Reimer averted

A note in a file from 1947 casts a potentially illuminating light on the relationship between Haarmann & Reimer and the National Socialist rulers. It refers to the fact that in 1940 the then employee Goseberg had applied to the responsible Reich office to aryanise two Dutch companies and have them taken over by Haarmann & Reimer. On 6 June, Dr. W.H./K. (probably Dr. Wilhelm Haarmann and Dr. Kerschbaum) wrote: "*Mr. Goseberg was in no way authorised to take this step and, thus, put the management in a very uncomfortable position. It should be noted in advance that the two gentlemen of the management, Dr. W. Haarmann and Dr. R. Haarmann, had to act with extreme caution in order to avoid damaging the company due to their previous membership of an association banned by the National Socialists in 1933, the Young German Order, and that they were only able to do so because Haarmann & Reimer was known among the population as one of the oldest companies in Holzminden and was popular due to the exemplary social care it provided to its employees.*" It also states that the management "*could not reject the negotiations initiated by Mr. Goseberg without further ado*", "*because this would have been immediately used by the party to accuse it of philosemitism*". Only when the proposal to take over the trusteeship together with the rival company Heine & Co was put forward, could the matter be rejected with "*good reason*". In the margin of the memo is the remark: "*Mr. Goseberg was dismissed by us on 31 May 1943.*"

Notification from the local court in June 1943: "*The power of attorney for Walter Goseberg, Holzminden, has been terminated*".

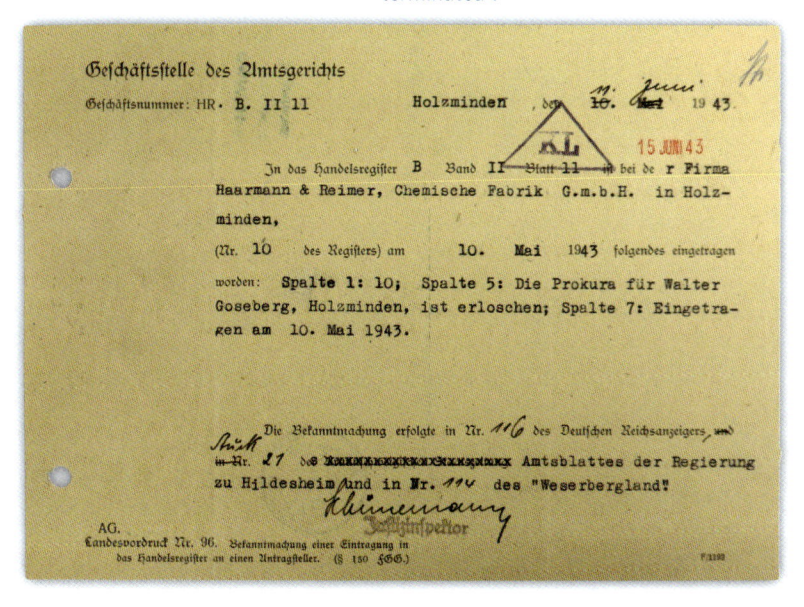

Reich grain silo
The construction of the grain silo on Weserkai between 1939 and 1941 gave Holzminden one of its most striking buildings to this day. The silo was built in the form of a 14-storey tower block. It was created as a visible, albeit camouflaged, symbol of the National Socialist self-sufficiency policy in the food industry in the event of war. At 55 metres high, it is still the tallest building in the town.

Heinrich Haensel price list from their anniversary year 1941

1941 – 100th anniversary Haensel

In 1941, Haensel, a Dragoco subsidiary, celebrated its 100th anniversary. The political developments of the 1930s and 1940s made the takeover of Haensel a stroke of luck for Dragoco, as domestic and artificial products became increasingly more important with the rise of National Socialist power in Germany. Fragrances and flavourings were not considered essential products for the war effort, but the importance of artificial flavourings, which were assigned to foodstuffs, increased during this period as the mood of the population and front-line soldiers could be lifted somewhat by tasty food, and because imported products were soon completely absent. It can be assumed that Heinrich Haensel's artificial beverage flavourings were very easy to market, especially in wartime and post-war times.

Dragoco in times of war

A copy of a letter from Carl Wilhelm Gerberding to District Leader Knop proves that the company most likely made good profits: "*As you know, I intended to use my company for war supplies at the beginning of the war and to forego any profit of any kind.*" This did not materialise because "*my company was not responsible for the deliveries in question (finished products made from raw materials).*" In view of the sacrifices that had been made in the meantime and as he was not in a position to serve his fatherland with arms or in the political field, "*I feel [...] compelled to make a special sacrifice at the end of the war year 1940. I am pleased to be able to do this after more than 20 years of work, which from the smallest beginnings has brought about a steady upward development of my company. With reference to the conversation we had, I am enclosing a crossed cheque for RM 20,000.*"

The transcript shows that Carl Wilhelm Gerberding also transferred 20,000 Reichsmark in December 1943, this time to "*District Leader Party Comrade Laue*" ("*Dear August!*") "*just as last time for charitable purposes for your district and for your personal disposal*".

The purchasing power parity table of the Deutsche Bundesbank shows that 20,000 RM would be equivalent to around €100,000 today.

With particular regard to the latter wording, it can be assumed that these monetary donations also served to appease the National Socialist political leaders who often acted locally in a high-handed manner.

In the 1970s, Gerhard Collin wrote in his chronicle: "*During the war years, Dragoco also produced perfume oils, although the processing plants of the pure perfumery industry were closed. It was necessary to convince the relevant Reich authorities that these 'perfume oils' also served other important purposes.*"

Furthermore, we can see from Gerhard Collin's notes that in 1944 the total turnover was made up as follows:

New Beginnings ...

"31.5% was supplied directly and indirectly to the armed forces,
30.6% was used in the context of orders from the Reich authorities, including the soap programme,
23.3% went to the food industry
and 16.6% was used by the pharmaceutical industry. Dragoco generates about 20% of its sales from exports of products not included in these quantities and values."
Collin explains that under certain conditions, exports to neutral countries were possible. Since Dragoco was partially dependent on the import of essential oils, there were clauses that, in turn, required the export of certain end products. Overall, Collin states: *"Despite all the war-related obstacles, it was possible to maintain a very extensive production programme and to supply the processing industry with all the products it needed."*

1943 – Wartime economy

On 3 December 1943, in a report on Haarmann & Reimer Chemical Factory of Holzminden, Paul Staude the then managing director and son-in-law of the company founder, describes the company's production to District Leader Laue (*"Dear Party Comrade Laue!"*). The report states that the base raw materials are subject to management *"for war-related reasons"*. *"In the case of H&R, the Reich Chemicals Department in Berlin is exclusively responsible for this, regardless of whether these raw materials are produced domestically or have to be sourced from abroad."* As far as the sales of Haarmann & Reimer products were to be reported, *"the reports for all fragrance sales, including vanillin and ethyl vanillin etc., went to the chemical industry economic group, and for all flavourings, i.e. aromas, to the food industry economic group."* Paul Staude goes on to explain that Haarmann & Reimer also produced flavourings from natural essential oils and other natural fruit extracts: *"H&R had to do without these additives more and more as the war went on; in future, the flavourings in question will be produced without any such additives or such products will be discontinued for the duration of the war."* Finally, the reporter emphasises: *"In all these cases, the Haarmann & Reimer products serve as aids for the fulfilment of production tasks to supply the Army or to cover civilian needs (subject to ration card)."*

Carbon copies of letters from Carl Wilhelm Gerberding about donations for "charitable purposes" from the years 1940 and 1943.

Haarmann & Reimer
chemische Fabrik zu Holzminden
G.m.b.H.

Bankkonten: Deutsche Bank, Berlin
Commerz- und Privat-Bank A.-G.,
Filiale Holzminden
Reichsbanknebenstelle Holzminden
Postscheckkonto No. 299 Hannover

Fernsprecher Nr. 619
Telegramm-Adresse: Vanillinfabrik Holzminden
A.B.C.-Code 5. Ausgabe - Lieber's Standard-Code
Carlowitz-Code - Rudolf Mosse-Code

Holzminden, den 21.8.1943

An das
Landeswirtschaftsamt

H a n n o v e r - O
Hinüberstrasse 4

St./K.

Betr.: Aufnahme kriegswirtschaftlich wichtiger Produktionen und Institute.

Wir bringen Ihnen pflichtgemäss zur Kenntnis, dass im Verfolg der im Einverständnis mit dem Rüstungsamt, Berlin, der Rüstungsinspektion XI a Hannover und den weiter eingeschalteten Behörden einschliesslich des zuständigen Kreisleiters nunmehr über alle bei uns aus kriegsbedingten Gründen nicht mehr voll ausnutzbaren Gebäude, Räume und Einrichtungen verfügt wurde. Dabei wurden alle Möglichkeiten der innerbetrieblichen Umstellung und des Austausches der für unsere eigenen kriegswichtigen Fertigungen benötigten Einrichtungen restlos ausgeschöpft.

Im einzelnen wurde zur Verfügung gestellt:

1.) Der Firma: B. Sprengel & Co., Hannover, Glünderstr. 8

    insgesamt rd. 300 m^2 Fabrikations- und Lagerraum

2.) dem Reichsinstitut für Erdölforschung an der Technischen Hochschule
                                                                         Hannover

    insgesamt rd. 300 m^2 Labor- und Lagerräume, sowie
    "   "   400 m^2 unbebaute Fläche für die Errichtung von Baracken für die gleichen Zwecke.

3.) der Firma: J.D. Riedel- E. de Haen A.G., Berlin-Britz

    für ihre verschiedenen Werke
    aller noch verbleibende Raum nebst Einrichtungen soweit er nicht für unsere eigenen schon erwähnten Produktionen dringend benötigt wird.

Die Vereinbarungen sind für 3.) -Riedel- bereits vertraglich unter dem 20.d.M. festgelegt. Für 1.) -Sprengel- und 2.) -Reichsinstitut- sind die Verträge in Bearbeitung.

In Sachen Riedel hat bereits die Rüstungsinspektion XI a, Hannover, die Sicherstellung auf Anordnung des Reichsministers für Bewaffnung und Munition -Rü Amt Nr. 16313/43/Rü II/4 A- unter dem 19.d.M. Z II verfügt.

Mit der Aufnahme der genannten zusätzlichen Produktionen und Laborarbeiten wird erklärlicherweise nunmehr die laufende Bereitstellung ausreichender Kohlenmengen erforderlich werden, ebenso dürfte sich ein erhöhter Energiebedarf (Fremdstrom) ergeben. Die Fragen bedürfen sicherlich einer eingehenden Aussprache. Wir werden uns erlauben, zu gegebener Zeit wegen des geeigneten Zeitpunktes dafür schriftlich evt. telefonisch Rückfrage zu halten.

                                        Heil Hitler!
                                Haarmann & Reimer
                              chemische Fabrik zu Holzminden, G.m.b.H.

                                                                                b.w.!

Letter dated 21 August 1943: Haarmann & Reimer informs the Hannover State Economic Office that *"facilities that can no longer be fully utilised"* will be made available to the companies Sprengel and Riedel-de Haën for *"production essential to the war effort"*.

1943 – Appropriation of the company premises

As a result of the bombing war on German cities, the Reich Institute for Petroleum Research was relocated from Hannover to the Haarmann & Reimer factory site in Holzminden in August 1943. Soon afterwards, further production facilities were 'secured' for the Riedel-de Haën company, which had been bombed in Berlin. In any case, a report to the British military government dated 4 December 1945 states: "*This confiscation would have paralysed us. However, through friendly negotiations with the Riedel company, we managed to retain part of our plant, which they did not necessarily need for their production, so that we were able to continue our production. In the meantime, the institute left us on 1 October 1945 and the Riedel-de Haën company on 1 November 1945.*"

It should be added that Haarmann & Reimer received rent payments from Riedel-de Haën despite the coercive measures and these helped it to survive the war. On the other hand, there were fears for some time that Riedel-de Haën might take over Haarmann & Reimer completely.

From Berlin to Holzminden: Stiebel Eltron

Dr. Theodor Stiebel invented the ring immersion heater and, in 1924, he founded the company which became well known and enjoyed rapid growth. During the Second World War, production was changed to armaments for the Luftwaffe. In the summer of 1943, the company moved production from the destroyed city of Berlin to Holzminden.
Hundreds of forced labourers were used to build the factory and produce the armaments.

Very few forced labourers

The forced labour lists for the Holzminden district, which are accessible via the Arolsen Archive International Centre on Nazi Persecution, provide a revealing picture of the companies' activities in the final years of the war. They show that Haarmann & Reimer and Dragoco each had two forced labourers working for them. The two French forced labourers at Dragoco are also mentioned in the memoirs of Carl-Heinz Gerberding. There were about a dozen at Riedel-de Haën. These are comparatively very small numbers and indicate that production in the final years of the war was quite low. In total, around 7,600 forced labourers were registered for the Holzminden district; two forced labourers was more common for nurseries or other small businesses.

1945 – Fatalities from bombing in Holzminden

During the bombing raid on Holzminden in April 1945, Gerberding's parents' house in Bahnhofstrasse was also hit. Luise Gerberding, mother of the company founder, died in the rubble, C.W. Gerberding himself was seriously injured. The house of Haarmann & Reimer chemist Dr. Tigges was also hit: In the report on the 1945 financial year, Wilhelm Haarmann Jr. wrote: "*Around 35 people who had taken refuge in the air-raid shelter of the house were killed, including Dr. Tigges himself with his daughter and her two children, our English correspondent, the Canadian Miss Margeret Scotland, and the wife of our chemist Dr. Hechelhammer with her two children.*" A total of 158 people died in Holzminden during the bombing raid on 3 April 1945.

Dr Wilhelm Haarmann jr.

A review of 1939 to 1945

In the report of 4 December 1945 to the British Military Government, already quoted in another context, Dr. Wilhelm Haarmann wrote on behalf of the management about the years 1939 to 1945: "*As a result of Germany being cut off from worldwide trade at the beginning of the war, the import of raw materials we obtained from overseas [...] was curbed. Due to this shortage of raw materials, production based on the processing of these materials gradually ceased. As the production of perfumeries and fine soaps was also severely reduced by the Reich government, sales in the fragrance department gradually declined. However, this loss was more than compensated for by the production and sale of artificial flavourings (aromas), the consumption of which increased in leaps and bounds due to the increased demand for instant custard, etc. [...]. From 1939 to 1941, sales increased steadily, in some cases considerably. The same applies to net profit.*"

As already mentioned, the reason for turnover declining in the further course of the war is largely due to the appropriation and renting of the production facilities for the Reich Institute for Petroleum Research from Hannover and Riedel-de Haën from Berlin.

Dr. Wilhelm Haarmann writes about the immediate post-war period that the company "*came through the several days of fighting around the Weser crossing near Holzminden [...] without major damage, so that after occupation they could start working again, once reasonable order had returned.*" He continued: "*In order to use our production facilities to their full potential, we have contacted the Berlin company Shering, whose factory has been destroyed, and will start manufacturing a series of products which are important in the pharmaceutical field, as soon as we are provided with sufficient coal for this purpose.*"

New Beginnings ...

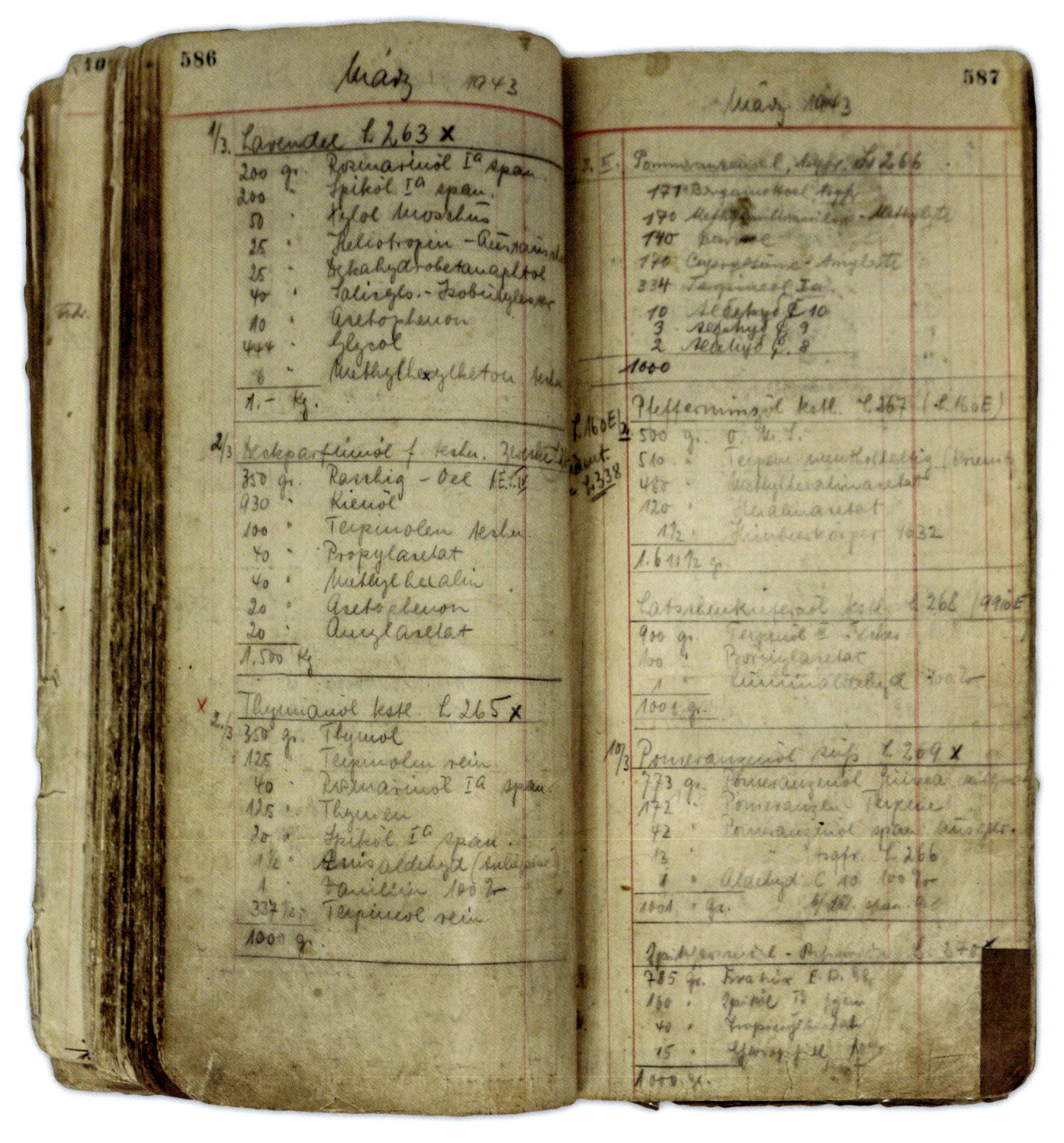

Haarmann & Reimer formula book from 1943: Due to the shortage of raw materials during this time, alternative formulas often had to be developed using the raw materials that were actually available.

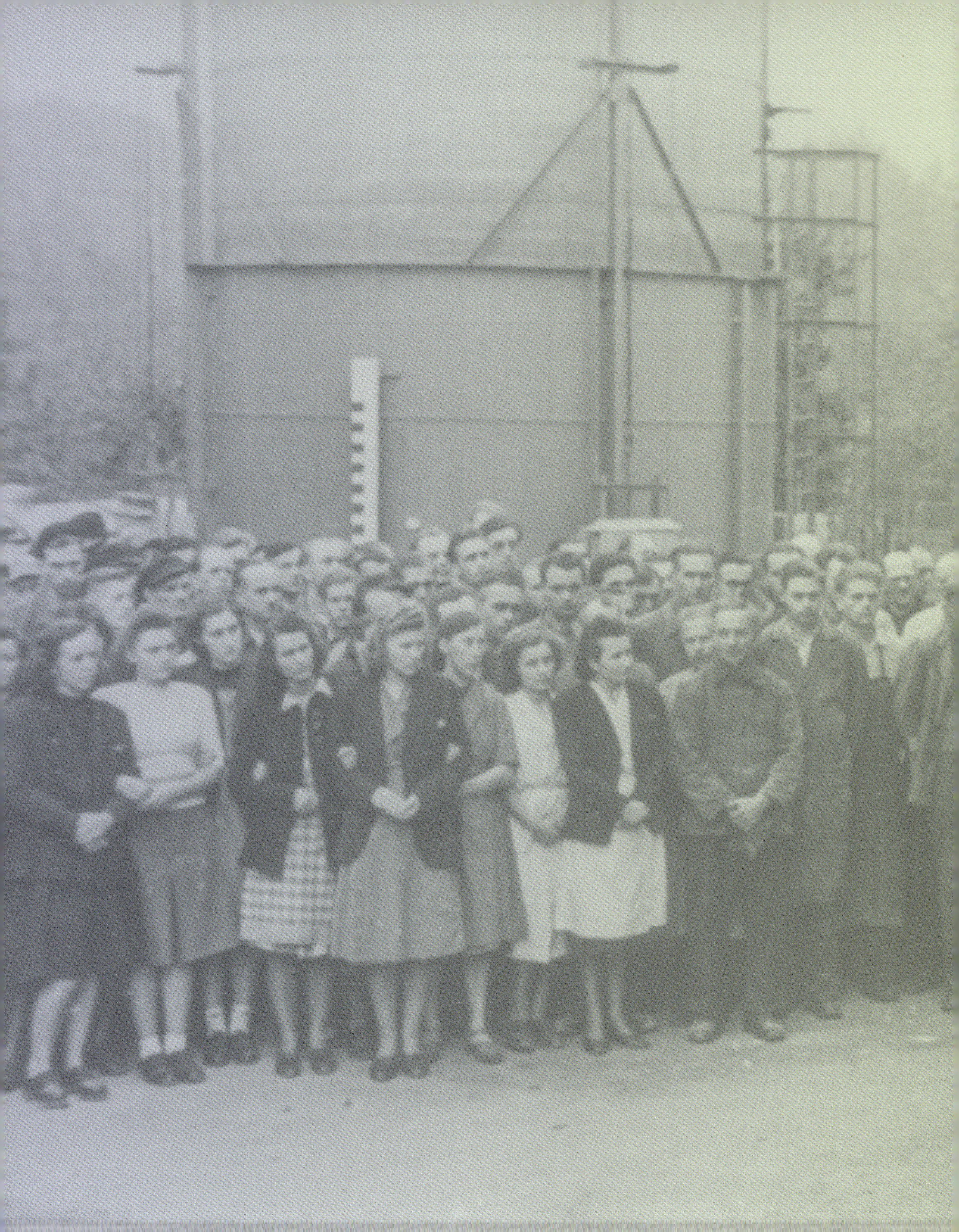

Dawn of the post-war period 1945 - 1955

WIRTSCHAFTSKAMMER HILDESHEIM

Hildesheim, den 10. Juli 1945
Waterloostraße 25

1a/Gü/Wa.

MILITARY GOV'T
1 7 JUL 1945
117 M.G. DET

Firma
Haarmann & Reimer
Chemische Fabrik zu Holzminden
G.m.b.H.

Holzminden/Weser

Betr.: Wiederaufnahme der Fertigung

Ihr Antrag vom: 15.6.1945

Im Auftrage der Militärregierung, 117. Det., erteilen wir Ihnen hiermit die Genehmigung zur Wiederaufnahme der Fertigung:

Herstellung von künstl. Riechstoffen für die Fabrikation von Seifen, Medikamenten, Desinfektionsmitteln usw., von Geschmackstoffen für die Lebensmittelindustrie sowie Herstellung von Lebensmitteln und Aushilfsstoffen für die Versorgung der Bevölkerung mit lebensnotwendigen Produkten mit bis 90 Kopf Belegschaft.

Die Militärregierung wünscht einen Bericht über den Stand der Wiederinbetriebnahme sowie eine Uebersicht über die geplante Fertigung. Deshalb ist sofort nach Betriebsbeginn ein entsprechender Bericht an die Wirtschaftskammer Hildesheim einzureichen, der folgende Angaben enthalten muß:

a) Zahl der Beschäftigten
   getrennt Arbeiter und Angestellte, männlich und weiblich, (getrennte Angaben nach Werkstätten, z. B. mechanische Werkstätten, Montage usw.) oder bei verschiedenen Fabrikationsprogrammen getrennte Angaben für einzelne Abteilungen z. B. Herdbau, Waschmaschinen, Öfen und dergl.

b) zu fertigende Erzeugnisse mit genauer Beschreibung und Angabe der Abmessungen und des Materials (z. B. bei der Geschirrfertigung Art des Geschirrs und Größe).

c) voraussichtlicher Materialbedarf bei Durchführung des geplanten Fertigungsprogramms (Bleche, Holz usw.)

d) voraussichtlicher Kohlen-, Strom-, Gas- und Wasserbedarf bei Durchführung des geplanten Fertigungsprogramms.

e) Lagerbestände an Fertigerzeugnissen aus der Fertigung vor der Besetzung.

f) Lagerbestände an vorhandenem Rohmaterial und Halbfabrikaten, die für das geplante Fertigungsprogramm verwendet werden sollen.

Soweit Ihr Betrieb auf die Zufuhr von Kohlen angewiesen ist, können Sie trotz dieser Genehmigung vorläufig nicht mit nennenswerten Zuweisungen rechnen.

Wir empfehlen Ihnen, zwecks Sicherung Ihres Betriebes bei dem örtlichen Kommandanten der Militärregierung ein «Off-limits»-Schild für Ihre Werksanlagen zu beantragen.

Wirtschaftskammer Hildesheim

CIV. MIL. GOV. OFFICER
(TRADE AND INDUSTRY)
117 (L/R) DET. MIL. GOV.

Hauptgeschäftsführer

Authorisation for the "*manufacture of artificial fragrances […], flavourings […] and the manufacture of foodstuffs and additives*" dated July 1949.

In the report on the 1945 financial year, Wilhelm Haarmann Jr. wrote: *"On 9 April 1945, Holzminden was occupied by the Americans. The population was deployed by the German authorities for clean-up work at the instigation of the American military government so that the factory had to be closed during the month of April. In May, we received permission from the American military government to continue working, which was confirmed several times by the British military government which replaced it a few weeks later. Essentially, goods which were scarce in the food and consumer industries were produced until transport to the outside world could be resumed by means of lorries that were soon deployed, and, thus, the sale of fragrance and flavouring products could gradually resume."* As the coal shortage continued, only small-scale production *"which consumes little steam"* could be carried out. Haarmann also wrote that stocks were now coming to an end and that production could not be resumed due to the lack of raw material imports. He continued: *"The two new divisions mentioned in the last report, 1. products for the retail trade / 2. pharmaceuticals, on the other hand, have developed well."* Haarmann also wrote that the company was in negotiations with the British military government to manufacture necessary products on a contract basis or under its own management. Turnover had fallen from around two million Reichsmarks in 1944 to around 1.5 million Reichsmarks in 1945.

Under the heading 'Outlook', Haarmann wrote: *"It is not yet possible to say today [27 June 1946] what the balance sheet result for the 1946 annual report will be. However, the new tax increases will absorb a substantial part of the profit. In addition, we will have to face a one-off levy on our assets. The management hopes to overcome this period of crisis, despite these heavy burdens, through the flexible management of production, sales and administration."*

In 1945, Haarmann & Reimer employed 32 white-collar workers and 37 blue-collar workers.

"Military government orders"' on issues relating to employee representation in the second half of the year

Minutes and results of the works council election of 1 June 1946

Holzminden, den 1.Februar 1946

Die ordnungsgemässe Betriebsrätewahl im Betriebe Haarmann & Reimer fand am 1.2.46 zwischen 4½ und 5 Uhr statt.
Von 54 Wahlberechtigten geben 50 = ca.93% ihre Stimmen ab.
An der Stimmenauszählung gemäß Anlage beteiligten sich der Wahlvorstand, die beiden Beisitzer und der Protokollführer.
Die Wahl verlief reibungslos und mit größtem Interesse.

I.A. [signature]
Protokollführer

Achtung ! Betriebswahlen !

Die ordnungsmässig vollzogene Betriebsratswahl hatte folgendes Ergebnis:

Es erhielten Stimmen:

1. Hanelmann, Aloys   34
2. Fuhrmann, Hermann   26
3. Immer, Karl   23
4. Diekmann, Otto   23
5. Kassebart Dr.Rolf   21
6. Esser, August   19
7. Ebeling, Wilhelm   16
8. Winnefeld, Else   16
9. Hillbrecht, Georg   13
10. Schmidt III Karl   8

Die erstgenannten 3 gelten als gewählte Betriebsratmitglieder, die nächsten 3 als ihre Ersatzleute.

Einsprüche sind innerhalb 7 Tagen, von heute gerechnet bis zum 9.Februar 1946 an die Militär-Regierung zu richten.

Holzminden, den 2.Februar 1946.

[signature] (Protokollführer)   [signature] (Wahlvorstand)

The Prince of Prussia as an apprentice at Dragoco

C.W. Gerberding's son Horst returned from the war injured, and his slightly older son Carl-Heinz returned physically unscathed. On 1 December 1945, the two sons and Prince Wilhelm Karl of Prussia joined Dragoco as apprentices. Prince Wilhelm Karl was actually an agricultural apprentice at the estate in Forst, but found accommodation with the Gerberdings in Victoria-Luise-Weg, where the family had found a new home after the destruction of the house in Bahnhofstrasse. In his memoirs, Carl-Heinz Gerberding describes his first encounter with Prince Wilhelm Karl in November 1945: *"This quiet morning hour was interrupted one day by the not entirely silent appearance of Wilhelm Karl. Until that moment, I had neither heard of nor seen him. Now he was there, sat down at the kitchen table without any fuss and, without saying a word, helped himself to plenty of food. We were used to all sorts of things, and only a few things could still astonish us, so we ate breakfast together, more or less in silence. The rest of the story is quickly told: Prince Wilhelm Karl came from some kind of soirée, as they used to say in those days. Most of the time it was just a noble get-together with his peers to forget the war and feel like he could get on with his life. It usually ended with a hangover that made some people hungry for something hearty. My early visitor was one of these people. After his work was done, he craved a Boonekamp, (a bitters), and, wonder of wonders, he knew exactly where to find one. We shared a drink and sealed a friendship that would last a lifetime."*

1946 – Manufacture of artificial or synthetic substances?

The newspaper *Welt* (founded in April 1946 in Hamburg by the British military government) published an article about the Holzminden fragrance companies by the journalist Dr. Mörtzsch at the end of 1946, and this led to an informative exchange of letters between Haarmann & Reimer and Dragoco about how the companies saw themselves and each other. After a visit by the journalist, C.W. Gerberding wrote to Haarmann & Reimer on 2 December 1946 that he had learned from a conversation with the journalist that Haarmann & Reimer was of the opinion that Dragoco *"did not manufacture standardised artificial fragrances"*, but that the company should rather be classified as a processing company in the industry. Gerberding made it clear in his letter *"that*

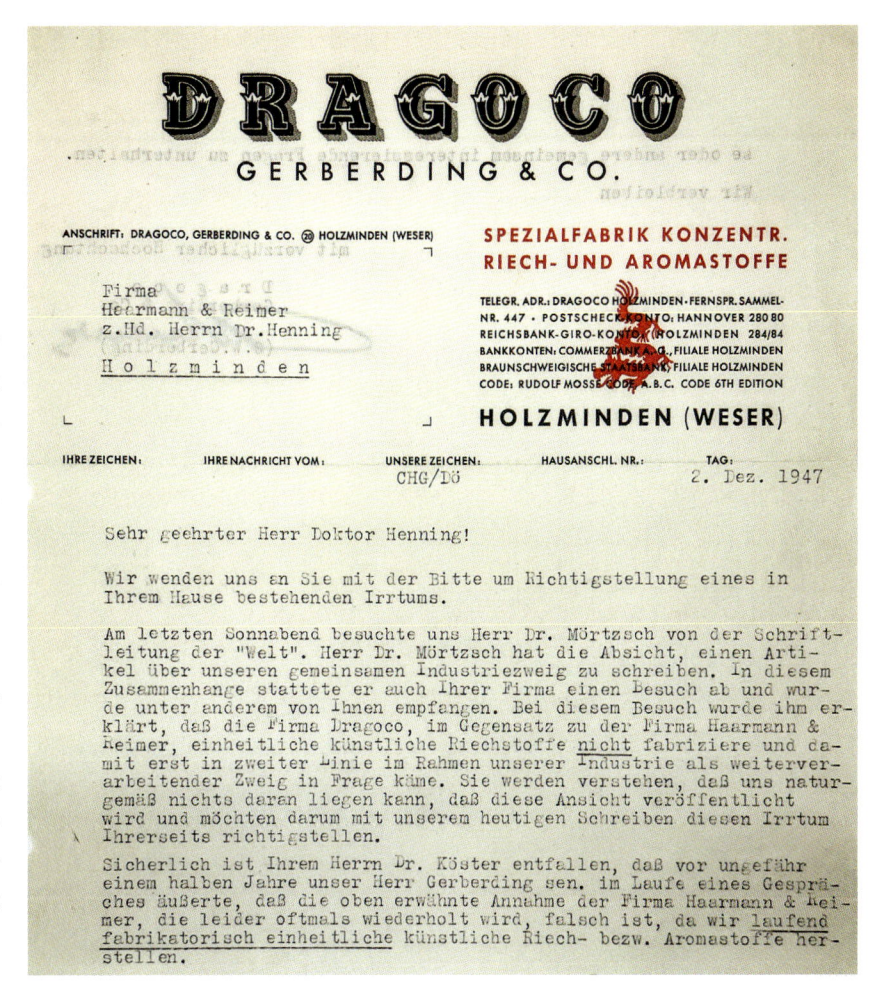

Letter from Carl Wilhelm Gerberding to Haarmann & Reimer dated 2 December 1947

the above-mentioned assumption of Haarmann & Reimer, which is unfortunately often repeated, is wrong, as we are constantly producing standardised artificial fragrances and flavours. [...] We have always had the wish to avoid clashes and unnecessary competition with their old traditional company. For this reason, we have deliberately refrained from producing certain standardised fragrances, such as those which are or were produced as specialities by Haarmann & Reimer, although it would be possible for us to do so. We would sincerely appreciate it if this letter could help to promote mutual understanding and would like to emphasise that we are still happy to discuss these or other questions of mutual interest with you."

In its reply, Haarmann & Reimer refers to a licence issued by the trade authorities in 1930, to which Gerberding replies again: "*In the 17 years that have passed, many things have naturally changed. Today, we continuously manufacture both standardised isolated fragrances and flavours from natural products, standardised artificial fragrances and flavours, as well as standardised synthetic fragrances and flavours. The necessary prerequisites are, of course, available. We hope that this information has cleared up any confusion.*"

With artificial tea products until the currency reform

With entrepreneurial fantasy, Dragoco succeeded in surviving the difficult years from 1945 to 1948. Among other things, artificial tea made from cheap nature-identical substances was produced to replace the lack of imports of natural tea.

Carl-Heinz Gerberding later wrote about the period after the currency reform in 1948: "*... and off we went. DRAGOCO also made rapid progress, no longer with hot drinks and tea substitutes, but with serious fragrances and flavours. Under father and uncle's* [August Bellmer] *management, a solid basis was created for a nationally orientated company. Without this sound foundation, the breakthrough into international business would hardly have been possible, or at least not so quickly.*"

A workforce of more than 300 employees in 1948 indicate that Dragoco apparently survived the Second World War much better than Haarmann & Reimer.

Advertising for Dragoco T-products from the post-war period

1949 – 30 years of Dragoco

The company celebrated its 30th anniversary in 1949. The photos from this event show that the times of hardship and hunger have clearly not yet been completely overcome. Nevertheless, the company management exudes confidence in a photo taken during the factory tour which was in keeping with the current favourable

Dragoco employees during a speech at the company's anniversary in 1949

The company management on a tour of the plant to mark the company's 30th anniversary: (from left) Horst Gerberding, August Bellmer, Senior Manager Carl Wilhelm Gerberding, Carl-Heinz Gerberding and authorised signatory Hermann Grossmann

economic development. Dragoco KG was transformed into a 'company under civil law'. In addition, a works fire brigade was founded, wisely it seems, as a photo album contains photos of fire damage in the company's original building, presumably from the 1930s.

1945 – 1955

Haarmann & Reimer staff anniversary celebration in 1947: Back row from left: Managing Director Wilhelm Haarmann jun.; Wilhelm Dormann, chemical production worker; August Heise, chemical production worker; Heinrich Diekmann, manager of the company health insurance; August Diekmann, warehouse manager; Carl Samse, chemical production worker. Front row from left: August Cromberg, warehouse manager; Wilhelm Probst, chemical production worker; Carl Klages, dispatch.

Haarmann & Reimer grows with great effort

On 20 August 1949, Haarmann & Reimer's 75th anniversary, a report on the first year after the currency reform of 20 June 1948 states: *"As can be seen from the balance sheet of 20 June 1948, the company entered the currency reform with cash and credit balances of over one million Reichsmarks. At the end, DM 60,000 remained from this balance. This amount was just enough to pay the wages and taxes payable in full in DM for June 1948."* After listing all the other problems that Haarmann & Reimer was facing, it went on to list the measures that were to be taken to overcome the situation: New recruits were *"Dr. Volpers (15.7.48) and Dr. Pirni (1.12.48) as junior chemists and Mr. Weber (1.1.49) as perfumer. In addition, the company has initially employed the chemist Dr. Laves, on a temporary basis; he comes from the Leuna plant and has relevant operational experience. Mr. Schwerdtfeger (1.9.48) and Mr. Helmut Steche (27.6.49) as purchasing staff. They are joined by the necessary support staff in the commercial and operational sectors. The aim of these appointments is to create further prerequisites for the resumption of research and development work and for the effectiveness of the company's sales organisation".* In addition, the company collaborated with external scientists for research, invested in the expansion and repair of company housing and in production facilities, machinery, the energy supply and means of transport. The report emphasises that no bank loans had to be taken out *"as turnover in the period*

Stenogramm-Übertragung
aus der Betriebsversammlung vom 24.Oktober 1947
an der teilgenommen haben:

1.) Der Betriebsratsvorsitzender Bessling,
2.) der Betriebsrat
3.) für die Geschäftsführung Dr.Henning und Dr.Reinh.Haarmann,
4.) fast die vollzählige Gefolgschaft.

I.

Der Betriebsratsvorsitzender Bessling eröffnete die Sitzung mit seiner Berichterstattung etc. lt. anliegendem Manuskript.

II.

Nach der Rede des B.Vors.Bessling ergriff auf Wunsch desselben Herr Dr.Henning das Wort:

Ich werde einen kleinen Überblick über die jetzigen Verhältnisse und jetzige Lage geben. Unsere Fabrik hat nach allen Seiten hin gute Geschäftsbeziehungen und es fällt nicht schwer, uns über Wasser zu halten. Wir liefern in der Hauptsache Aromen und was wir liefern, ist noch Vorkriegsqualität zu Vorkriegspreisen. Wir stehen haushoch über Alle. Es fehlen uns nur Rohstoffe, in der Hauptsache ausländische Rohstoffe, aber wir helfen uns andererseits mit allen möglichen Produktionen. Dieser Zustand ist allerdings nicht von Dauer. Wir merken heute schon, dass eine Geldknappheit eingesetzt hat, sodass wir nicht mehr so verkaufen wie früher. Wir müssen unser Augenmerk auch auf die kommende Geldwährung richten und wenn die Geldwährung eingesetzt hat, werden wir alle unsere Kräfte daran setzen, dass wir an Deck bleiben. Wir sind das ärmste Land und müssen aus Trümmern aufzubauen versuchen und das werden wir auch tun. Ein Jeder von uns wird das Allerbeste hergeben und wir Alle werden alles daran setzen, um die Chemie aufzubauen. Wir werden unsere Apparaturen pflegen und an allen Orten äusserste Ordnung halten. Wir tuen das nicht etwa, weil wir einen Schönheitsfimmel haben, sondern wer die Ordnung hält, braucht nie nach seinen Sachen zu suchen, sondern er braucht dann nur zu greifen und es ist da. - Wie war das früher? Vor dem Kriege hatten wir über die Hälfte unserer Produkte exportiert. Die Geschäftsführung hat sich die grösste Mühe gegeben, wieder in dieses Exportgeschäft hineinzukommen. Das ist aber verdammt nicht leicht. - Es sind hier und da Leute aufgetaucht, die sich plötzlich selbständig gemacht haben und uns so Konkurrenz machen. Dann ist ein weiteres Übel aufgetaucht, das ist der Papierkrieg. Sie können sich hiervon keine Vorstellung machen. Ein Wust von Papier muss oft bewältigt werden um den Wünschen und Fragen der Mil.Reg. Rechnung tragen zu können.
Ich sage noch einmal, wir möchten gerne exportieren, eben weil wir später darauf angewiesen sein werden und wir werden uns alle Mühe geben, nur so wird es allgemein vorangehen, wenn wir uns allesamt anstrengen. Ausländische Produkte sind nicht abzusetzen, dazu sind wir zu arm in Deutschland. So haben wir auf Synthesen etc. zurückgreifen müssen. Unsere Herren Chemiker sind eifrig bei Entwicklungsarbeiten beschäftigt und mit aller Intensivität sind wir bemüht, neue Produkte aufzunehmen. Nur derjenige weiß, wie es in der Geschäftswelt aussieht, der heute in Deutschland rumfährt. Und ich kann nur sagen, wir müssen gute Arbeitskräfte haben, darum nehmen wir neue Handwerker an und neue Leute, die wir anlernen.
Eins muss ich noch sagen, die Produkte, welche früher nur durch

-2-

Stenogram transmission (part 2 on page 92) from the works general meeting on 27 October 1947. The term 'Gefolgschaft' (followers) is used several times indicating that the rule of the National Socialists had obviously not yet been overcome linguistically.

eine Postkarte zu haben waren, sind heute sozusagen unerreichbar, weil unsere früheren Lieferanten zum Teil in der Ostzone sitzen und zum anderen Teil die Fabriken durch Bomben vernichtet sind. Auf der anderen Seite aber sind hier und da Einzelwerke entstan= den, die sich auf unser Gebiet stürzen. Ich finde diese Herren viel vor auf meinen Reisen und das alles sagt, dass wir uns enorm anstrengen müssen. Wir gehen dabei davon aus, dass die Firma uns trägt und darum müssen wir zusammenhalten und nicht nur für das Heute sondern auch für das Morgen sorgen. Wir könnten allerdings, wie es schon viele tun, auf dem Schwarzmarkt kaufen und verkaufen, aber das tuen wir nicht, sondern wir schlagen uns schon durch, darum muss jeder wissen, dass es auf seinen Fleiss und auf seine Zuverlässigkeit und Pünktlichkeit ankommt. Wir werden alle nach besten Kräften zugreifen und für unsere Firma schaffen, um uns so die Zukunft zu sichern. Haben Sie nur das Vertrauen zu der Geschäftsführung, so wird diese das gleiche Vertrauen zu Ihnen haben.

III.

Herr B.-Vors.Bessling dankte für den Vortrag des Herrn Geschäfts= führers Dr.Henning.

IV.

Der B.-Vors.Bessling ergriff von neuem das Wort zur Tagesordnung: Er erwähnte die Einrichtung einer Werksküche.
Gefolgsch.Mitglied Taube erklärte: Ich bin der Ansicht, dass Alle die auswärts wohnen bestimmt an der Werksküche teilnehmen werden, aber wie ist es mit der Abgabe von Lebensmittelkarten?
B.-Vors.Bessling: Es wird sehr wenig sein, was an Lebensmittelmarken abzugeben ist.
 Es meldeten sich 23 Gefolgschaftsmitglieder, die f ü r die Einrichtung einer Werksküche waren, 51 dagegen.

V.

Dann bat Dr.Kassebart ums Wort: Auf die Verteilung von Syrup etc. zurückzukommen, schlage ich folgendes vor:
Der Ledige erhält eben in Zukunft nur 1¼ kg und der Verheiratete entsprechend mehr. Genau so kann mit den Einmachgläsern und Kon- serven-Dosen und Deckeln verfahren werden.
 Auf diesen Vorschlag hin erfolgten unter der Gefolgschaft sofort Widerrufe.
Der B.Vorsitzende Bessling griff auch sofort mit folgenden Worten ein:
 Ich möchte weiterhin den Grundsatz der Geschäftsführung und auch den meinigen vornehmen, nämlich, dass jeder der hier arbeitet dasselbe Quantum an Syrup undsoweiter erhält, wie es bisher gehandhabt wurde. Ich sehe nicht ein, warum der Ledige weniger erhalten soll, als der Verheiratete und somit nur bestraft wird, weil er nun mal noch ledig ist. Ich bin selbst verheiratet und habe 2 Kinder, kann aber trotzdem die Ansicht von Herrn Dr.Kassebart nicht teilen.
Daraufhin bat Herr R.A.Kerschbaum ums Wort: Auch ich kann die Ansicht von Herrn Dr.Kassebart nicht teilen und dies ist auch, soviel wie ich weiss nie und nimmer die Ansicht der Geschäfts= führung. Vielmehr ist der Sinn der Geschäftsführung, dass jede Arbeitskraft, die hier bei uns arbeitet, seinen Teil erhält. Gewiss ist das sehr schön, wenn der Verheiratete nach Hause kommt und die Kinder grosse Augen machen. Ich bin heute selbst verheiratet muss aber sagen, ich weiss, was das heißt, gerade in der heutigen Zeit als Lediger sich redlich durchzuschlagen; (Hierauf erfolgten laute Bravorufe und großer Beifall) eben weil ich selbst ungefähr 8 Jahre lang als Lediger draußen war.

from the currency reform to 31 July 1949, i.e. in 13 1/3 months, amounted to around DM 4,840,000. However, the company's liquid assets had to be stretched to the limit".

The Symrise archives also contain a *"first rough draft"* of a report to the supervisory board dated 7 December 1949 on the reporting period from August to November 1949, which speaks of a decline in sales due to the fact that *"as a natural reaction against the many artificial war and post-war goods in Germany, a considerable aversion to all synthetic flavourings is becoming increasingly noticeable as the supply of natural essences increases. […] We are feeling the effects of this trend particularly in the beverage industry. But custard powder manufacturers are also currently favouring the chocolate-cocoa direction using the natural product. Moreover, as far as vanillin flavourings are concerned, lignin vanillin from the USA is being offered on the domestic and foreign markets in considerable quantities."*

The picture shows a Haarmann & Reimer trade fair stand in 1949, the year in which the company celebrated its 75th anniversary.

The two Holzminden companies in 1950

To mark the opening of Holzminden's Weser Bridge in October 1950, a commemorative publication was published in which author Fritz Olms presented Holzminden's businesses under the title Holzminden, the up-and-coming industrial town. It states: *"The chemical industry is of significant importance for the economic and social structure of the town, can be described as crisis-proof and is probably the best taxpayer. The oldest company of this type and also the oldest plant in Germany is HAARMANN & REIMER GMBH. Holzminden can, therefore, be considered the birthplace of today's flavour and fragrance industry."* It continues: *"At present, the company is successfully endeavouring to regain connection to the world market which was lost during the Second World War. Before the war, 60% of production went abroad. The factory operates laboratories, research and production facilities on a site complex of 23,000 square metres. The factory offers 226 families a rewarding and secure existence; 116 factory-owned flats are available and this is being increased. The social care of the employees is exemplary. The order and production situation is good, but is currently being curbed and inhibited by a shortage of raw materials on the world market due to the Korean crisis."*

Fritz Olms writes the following about the second Holzminden-based fragrance company: *"DRAGOCO GMBH is the largest specialised factory in the fragrance and flavour industry in the Federal Republic of Germany. Founded in 1919 by Mr. C. W. Gerberding and Mr. A. Belmer as a special factory for concentrated fragrances and flavours, this plant has experienced a rare steep rise despite the economic crises of the last 30 years and today employs a workforce of 350. […] However, the company can take lasting credit for the new fragrances it has created through painstaking scientific research, which have made a significant contribution to developing the name Dragoco into a world-famous and global term for high-quality and modern fragrances and flavours."*

The commemorative publication marking the opening of the new bridge provides a good overview of economic life in Holzminden in 1950.

1945 – 1955

Haarmann & Reimer's fleet in the 1940s

Address details from a Dragoco price list from the 1950s

Schimmel price list, Hamburg

Upswing with refugees and skilled workers from the East

In 1952, Dragoco already had 450 employees. In his review, Prince Wilhelm Karl of Prussia spoke at the '75 years of Dragoco' celebrations: "*For younger people today, it is hard to imagine the millions of homeless people and refugees who once again travelled through Germany. In search of their families, food and a roof over their heads - and work. Carl Wilhelm Gerberding took in far more of them at Dragoco than were needed for the small volume of business in those days. [...] The people concerned thanked him with loyalty and company loyalty. [...] But I must mention another gift of the company founder that had a considerable influence on Dragoco's development: since bad things almost always have a good side and it is part of the art of life to notice and, above all, make use of this, the flight of our industry's specialists from the Soviet-controlled factories in the Leipzig area, which had formed the heart of the industry for decades, proved to be a great reservoir of expertise for the local region. Carl Wilhelm Gerberding made use of it. Unfortunately, the 'business revitalising' competition also made use of such opportunities, and this occasionally resulted in a competition that was as noble as it was adventurous.*"

But not only were skilled workers poached from the traditional companies in the fragrance industry in the Leipzig area, the Holzminden companies also took over offshoots and branches of these companies in Western Europe: Haarmann & Reimer, which already had business relations with Schimmel & Co through the vanillin consortium, took over the Schimmel branch in Hamburg in 1952. The company used this business to continue selling its own products under the Schimmel name for many years to come. And as 'unnoticed' as possible. The name Haarmann & Reimer is not mentioned in a brochure to mark the 125th anniversary of Schimmel & Co. The brochure states: "*The last world war also became the fate of our company. The Russian occupation was followed by the expropriation of the Miltitz factory, which was declared a state-owned enterprise. After meeting the very difficult legal requirements, the company's registered office was relocated to Hamburg in 1950 and production was then resumed. Old Miltitz employees soon came together again in Hamburg to actively and purposefully help rebuild their original factory.*"

In 1959, Dragoco acquired the Schimmel sales office in Austria. Schimmel Vienna became a hub for exports to the Comecon countries of Eastern Europe and the good name of Schimmel & Co also opened the door to numerous new customers for Dragoco.

Dawn ...

Dragoco – the largest and most modern company

The new administration and laboratory building on Dragocostrasse was officially opened in 1950. This building still dominates Symrise's Solling plant today.

In the publication *Köpfe und Kräfte, Band 1: Aus der Wirtschaft Niedersachsens*, (Heads and Strengths, Volume 1: From the Lower Saxonian Economy), Carl Wilhelm Gerberding's company, Dragoco – Speciality factory for concentrated fragrances and aromas – Holzminden, is presented under the heading *Der Mann und sein Werk* (The Man and his Work). The report makes it clear that Dragoco, together with the integrated company Heinrich Haensel, had developed into a competitor, also in the scientific field, which was on a par with the traditional company Haarmann & Reimer. After a description of the various production facilities, it says: *"Of particular importance is the large-scale production of pure,*

Carl Wilhelm Gerberding, c.1950

Quality control, c.1960

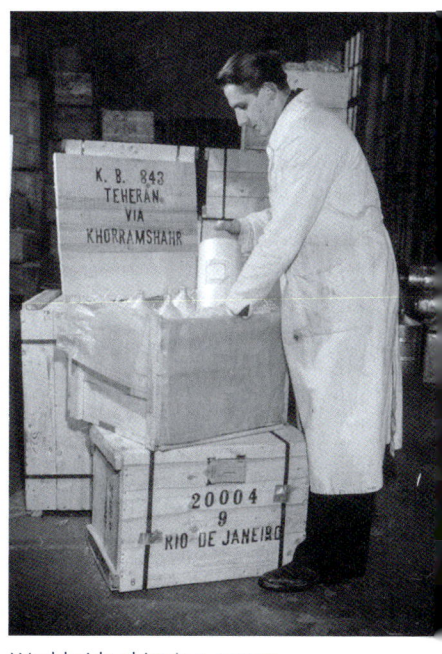

Worldwide shipping, c.1950

1945 – 1955

End of work in the 1950s. Employees leave the Dragoco factory premises through the gate to Liebigstrasse.

Cover picture of a Heinrich Haensel brochure on liqueur extracts, and a Dragoco brochure both from the 1950s

Dawn ...

Above: Dragoco brochure entitled 'raw menthol or pure menthol' (cover picture see p 98) from the 1950s.

Right: As early as 1955, the Dragoco factory premises were extended with building 15 in the direction of the Solling along Wiesenweg.

Below: flavour production at Dragoco in the 1950s

1945 – 1955

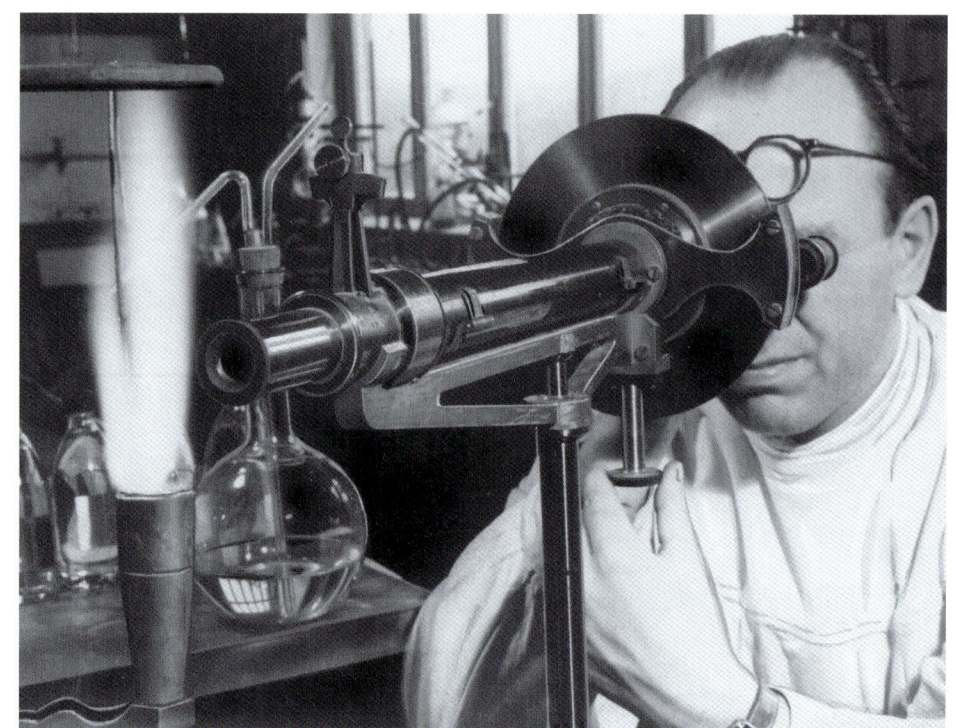

Dragoco researcher
Dr. Farnow

Menthol production at Dragoco

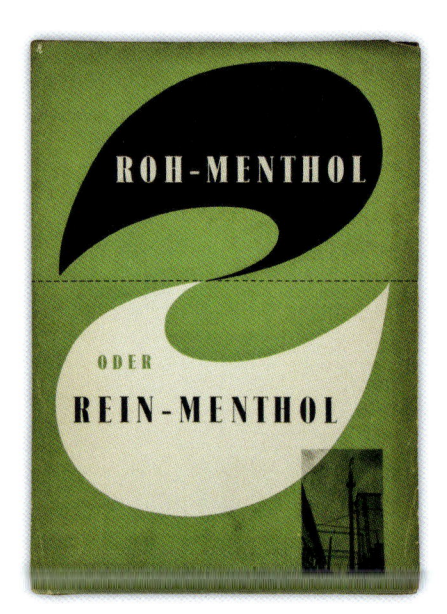

natural menthol, which occurs in another newly constructed factory building and whose output is able to cover the entire demand of the Federal Republic of Germany and helps to save foreign currency previously spent on the considerable import of the product from China, Japan or Brazil, and even enables the company to export it itself. The atmosphere is completely different in the corridor which stretches over 80 metres and provides a view into around two dozen research and development laboratories to the right and left, where highly qualified scientists work on current problems, almost in silence and cut off from the world, with fine and sophisticated precision equipment at their disposal. Here, in close collaboration with the 1950 Nobel Prize winner for chemistry, Prof. Dr. Kurt Alder, work is carried out on the continuous development of synthetic fragrances and flavours under the supervision of renowned chemists from Germany and abroad."

In conclusion, it emphasised that in just 33 years, the company had grown from its founder Carl Wilhelm Gerberding to become the *"largest and most modern company in the fragrance and flavour industry in the Federal Republic of Germany"*. In 1955, the company built a factory canteen for its now more than 500 employees, and in the following years the factory premises were extended eastwards along Wiesenweg.

1954 – Takeover by Bayer

After a lengthy restructuring process, Haarmann & Reimer was acquired by Bayer and managed as an independent subsidiary. Bayer had transferred the business of the Agfa fragrances division to Haarmann & Reimer as early as 1953.

A speech on the occasion of Haarmann & Reimer's 80th anniversary stated: *"The factory extends over an area of 15 acres. As you can see at first glance, there are still a number of clear spaces between the individual buildings, but these also have their significance. Firstly, we intend to thoroughly develop and remodel our plant in the very near future and also to enlarge it considerably; and secondly, we need a lot of storage space for the numerous materials."*

The colour photos on this page show the Haarmann & Reimer factory premises in the 1950s and early 1960s. Most of the buildings and facilities date from before the First World War. With Bayer's capital, the buildings and production facilities of Haarmann and Reimer were completely renovated in the following years.

1945 – 1955

In addition to the expansion of the plant, numerous international subsidiaries were founded. The sale to Bayer also marked the end of the Haarmann family's 80-year connection to the company because the family members sold their shares.

A note on the back of the colour photo above reveals that these workers were transporting menthol.

Right: Haarmann & Reimer laboratory in the 1950s

Below: site plan from 1958 showing planned construction

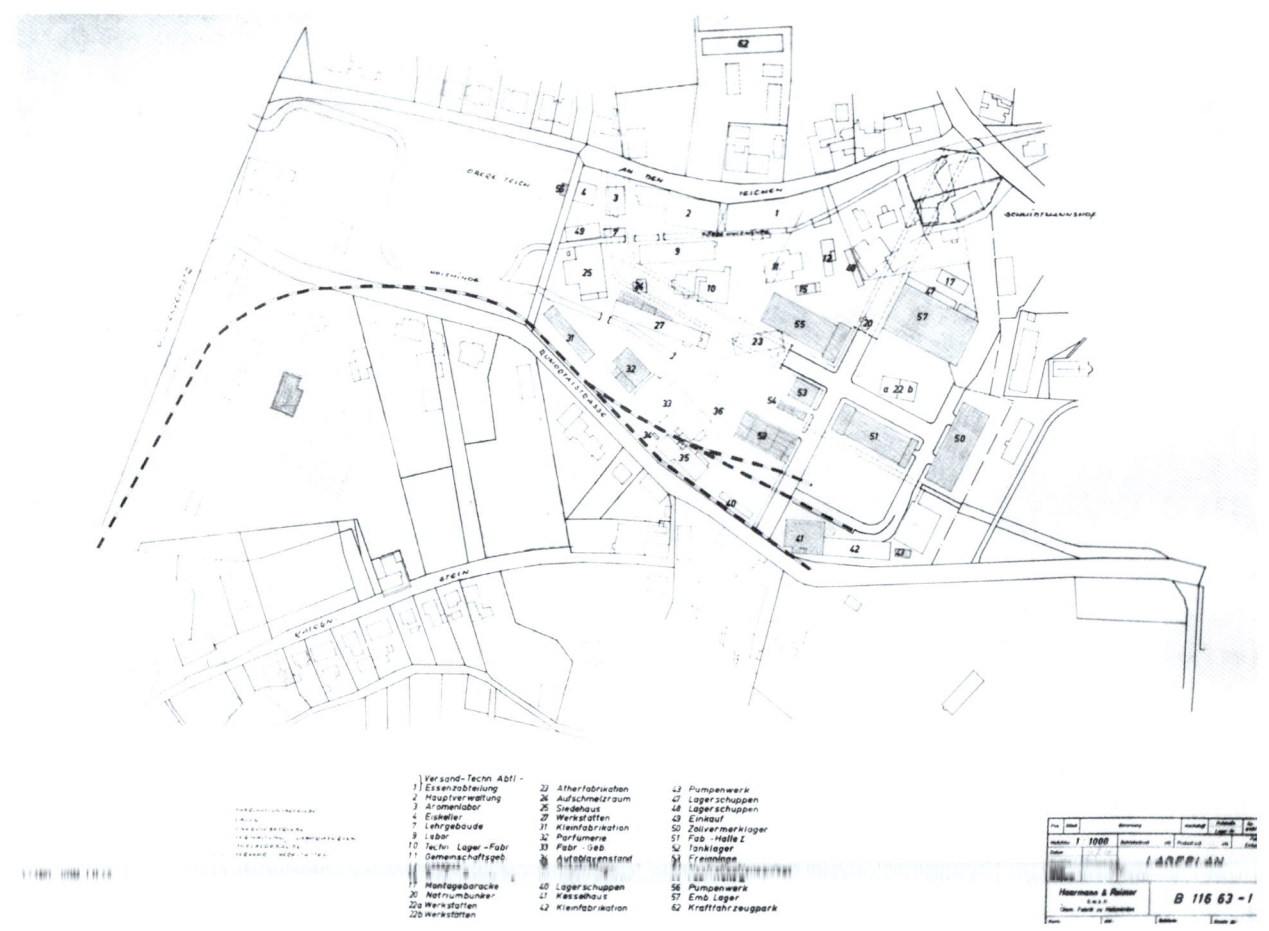

Dawn ...

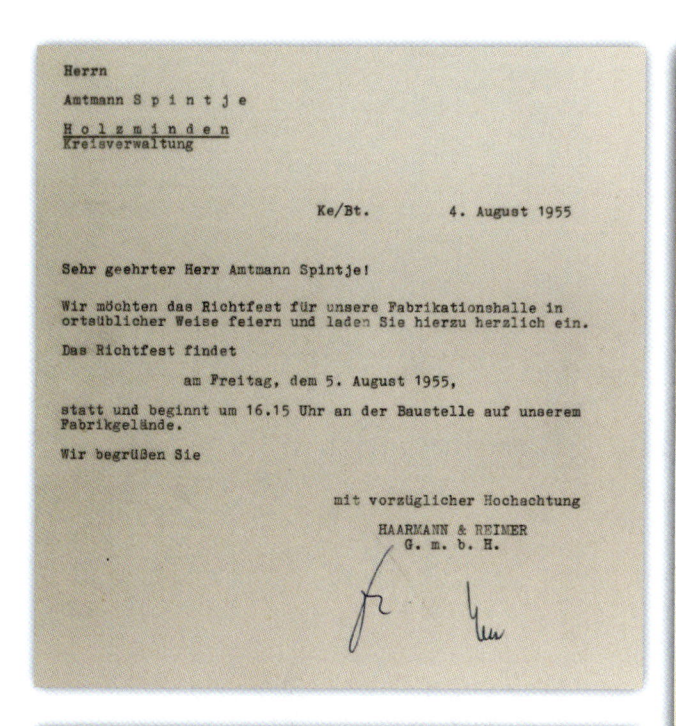

Above: invitation, schedule and newspaper report on the topping-out ceremony for the new production building in August 1955
Below: photo of the finished building and aerial view of the Haarmann & Reimer factory premises at the end of the 1950s

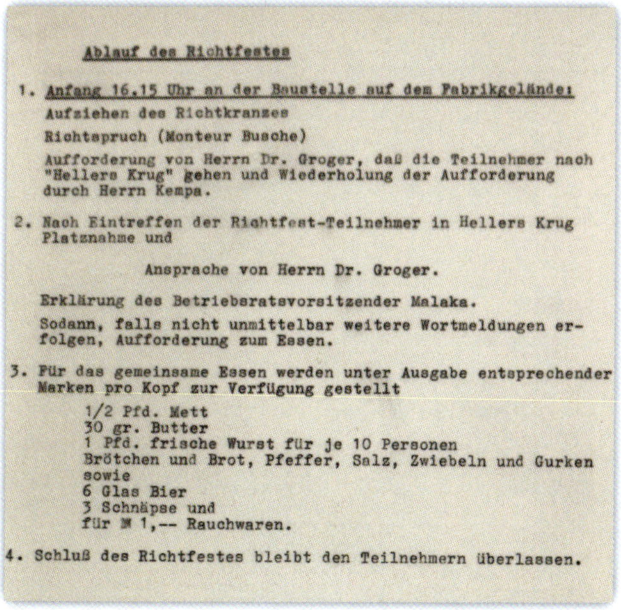

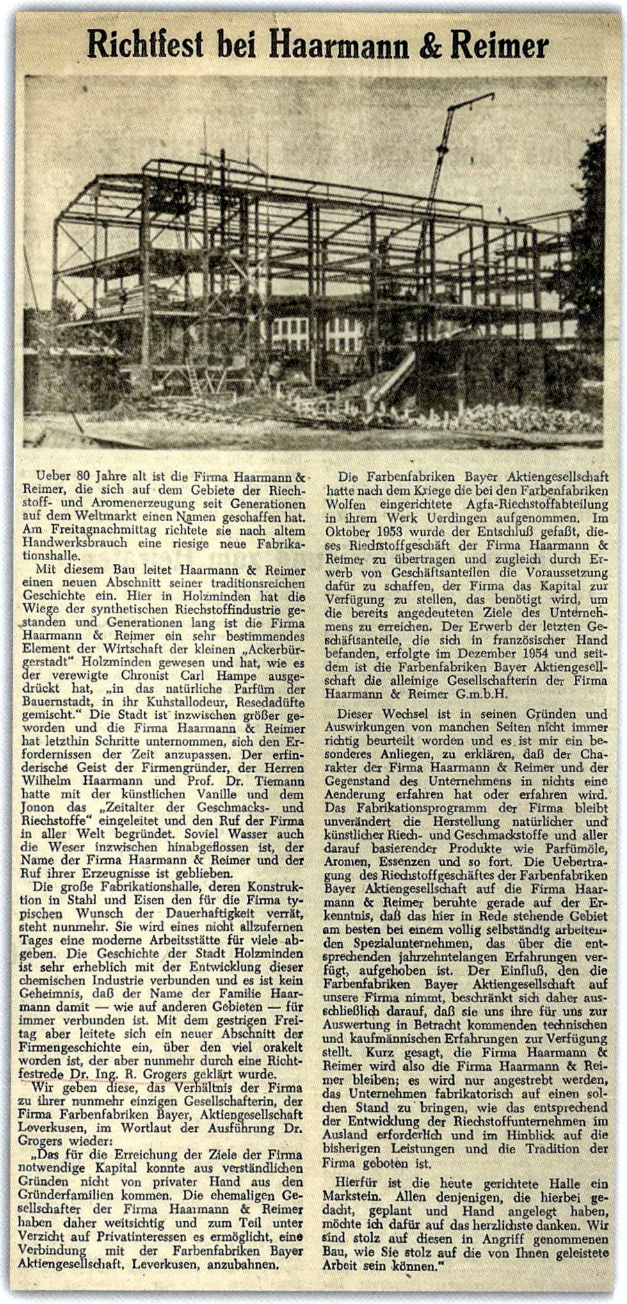

1945 – 1955

Other fragrance and flavouring companies

In the post-war period, a number of similar companies were founded in the vicinity of the two large Holzminden fragrance and flavouring companies Haarmann & Reimer and Dragoco. In the 1950s and 1960s, Bohnsack & Goseberg, later renamed Goseberg & Co; and Gustav Nowak's company Novarom gained some importance.

Price list from 1951

Bohnsack & Co. headquarters on Sollingstrasse, c.1960

Picture taken of production, c.1960

Bohnsack & Goseberg

Bohnsack & Goseberg GmbH (BOGO) was founded in Sollingstrasse back in 1946. BOGO produced flavour concentrates, liqueur and delicatessen essences and oils. The founders of the company were former senior employees of Haarmann & Reimer. The Symrise archives contain evidence that Walter Goseberg's power of attorney had expired on 10 May 1943 and that of chemist Dr. Heinrich Bohnsack on 2 February 1944. It was obvious they had parted on bad terms.

In connection with the political consequences of the First World War, Gennermann's book Eine Geschichte mit Geschmack (A History With Taste) quotes from the minutes of the Vanillin Convention regarding the deliberations to establish a Belgian syndicate in 1935: *"Brussels is not an option as a place of consultation, as Mr. Goseberg from Haarmann & Reimer seems to have made himself so popular there during the war that he still has to fear immediate arrest if he crosses the border."* This remark relates to war crimes committed by German troops in 1914. Of the 900 people who were tried in the Leipzig trials for German war crimes during the First World War, only ten were convicted. These trials were seen as a farce in Belgium and France, where hundreds of Germans were sentenced to death in absentia; Goseberg was apparently among those convicted. It is also clear from other documents [see p. 75] that Haarmann & Reimer was not happy with the behaviour of its employee Goseberg.

In 1950, the company was described in the commemorative publication marking the official opening of the bridge as follows: *"Managed by highly skilled specialists, the company's activities range from the production of flavours, concentrates, extracts, liqueur essences and distillates to essential oils and fragrances. Until recently, the company has been housed in temporary facilities in several locations around the town due to time restraints. However, it has now succeeded in taking over a factory complex so that all parts of the company are combined and there is now the possibility of further expanding the business. [...] The workforce currently consists of 25-30 people."*

A little later, Walter Goseberg left the company, which continued as Bohnsack & Co. In 1968, the company was finally taken over by Haarmann & Reimer.

Other Companies

Novarom

Novarom was founded by former Dragoco employee Gustav Adolf Nowak in 1966, initially under the name Aroflor. The company was initially based at Gehrenkamp 44, where small batches of cosmetic additives were produced in a garden shed. In 1972, the company was renamed Novarom and it moved to its newly built production facilities in Birkenweg in Bevern. At the beginning of the 1980s, the company headquarters were further expanded.

According to the commercial register, the object of the company was *"the sale and manufacture of chemical products of all kinds, in particular fragrances and flavourings, raw materials, additives and active ingredients for the cosmetics and pharmaceutical industries, as well as the wholesale and retail of such and product-related items"*. However, the focus was probably on cosmetic products, as Gustav Adolf Nowak had also made a name for himself as an author with his specialised publication: *Die kosmetischen Präparate Rezeptur, Herstellung und wissenschafltliche Grundlagen* (Cosmetic Preparations, Formulation, Manufacture and Scientific Principles). It was first published in 1969 and developed into a standard work that was reissued in revised editions until the early 1990s.

Novarom was taken over by the British company Croda in 1991. Wikipedia states: *"In 1991, with the acquisition of Novarom, which was renamed Crodarom in 1998, the company was able to produce plant and plant extracts using new extraction techniques."*

Today, parico cosmetics, the export and distribution company, offers plant-based cosmetic products under the brand name Novarom.

The production site in Bevern, managed by Croda, continued to operate until the 2000s. The premises on Birkenweg were then taken over by the cosmetics manufacturer Güldenmoor.

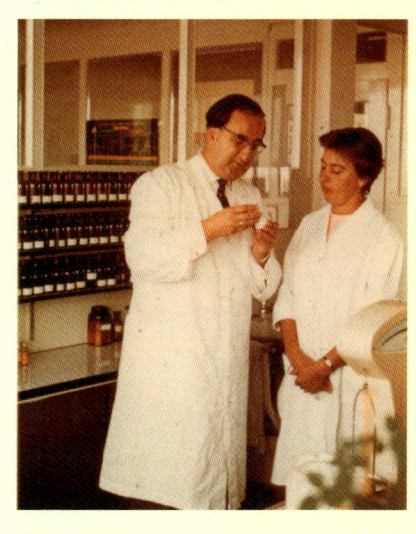

Gustav Adolf Nowak

Perfume formula, handwritten by Gustav Adolf Nowak

Goods being loaded at the company premises on Birkenweg, Bevern

Other Companies

VERONA-PHARMA
CHEMICAL CORPORATION
HAARMANN & REIMER
CORPORATION

Worldwide Growth 1956 - 2002

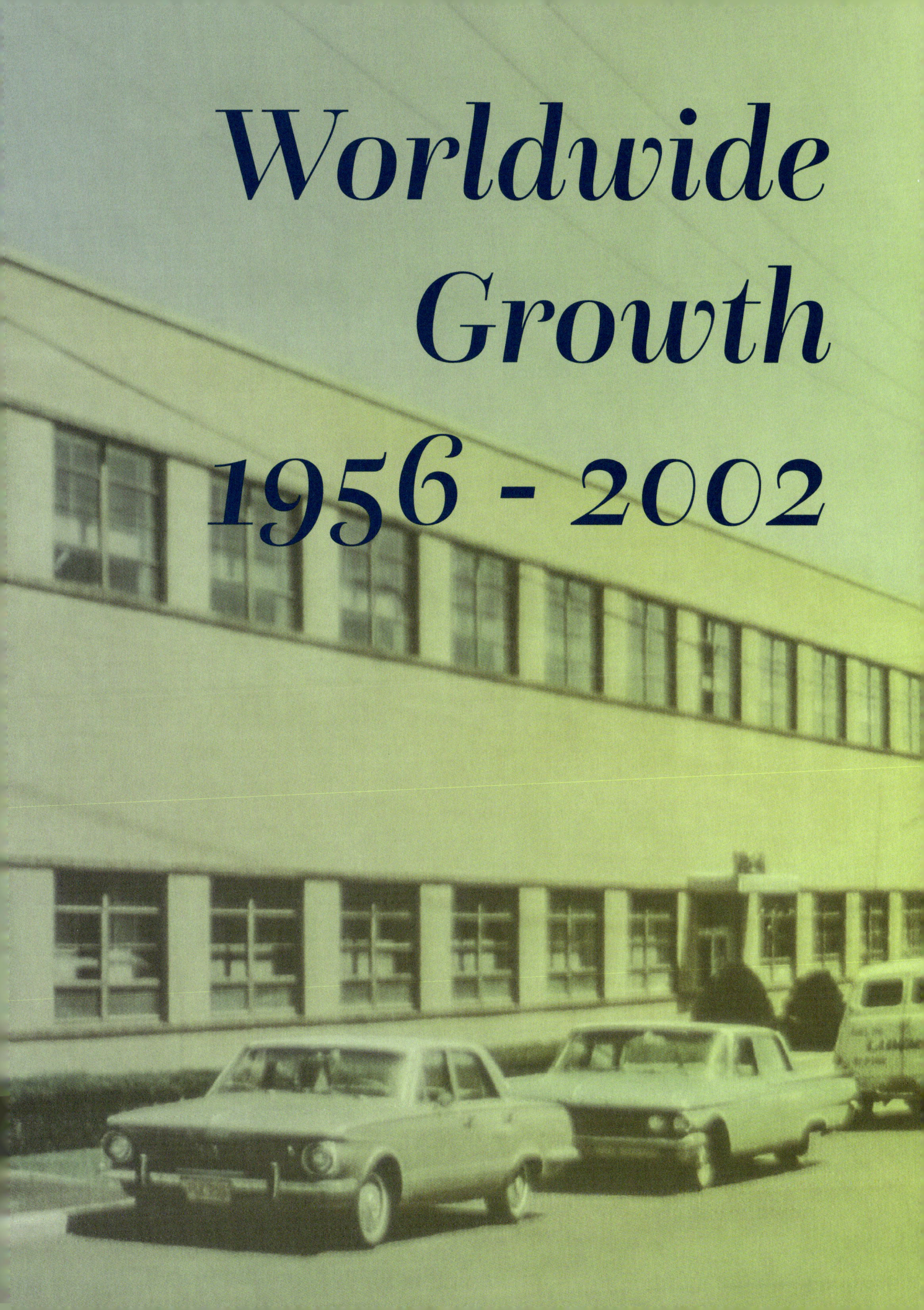

The two aerial photos of Dragoco's premises from 1956 (top) and 1958 (bottom) illustrate how quickly the company was developing at the time. In the bottom picture, the canteen, which had just been completed, can be seen on the far right and new buildings have also been erected in the centre of the factory premises and on the left-hand side of the picture.

Worldwide Growth

As the previous chapter has shown, although the Holzminden fragrance and flavour industry was initially hard hit by the Second World War, it was primarily able to benefit from the loss of the once leading fragrance and flavouring companies in the Leipzig area; on the one hand by recruiting skilled workers who had fled; and, on the other, by taking over branches located in the areas under the influence of the West.

In doing so, the companies in Holzminden created a very good starting position for the so-called 'economic miracle years' that followed in Germany. Although the Korean crisis of 1950-53 with its global economic repercussions put a slight damper on things, it strengthened the young Federal Republic's integration into 'the West' and ultimately boosted its foreign trade. As early as 1952, the Federal Republic was exporting more than it was importing. In the following years, the two major fragrance companies in Holzminden set up and expanded their branches all over the world.

Symbol of the building boom during the German economic miracle: chimney construction at Dragoco

1956 – Dragoco founded subsidiary in the USA

From the mid-1950s, C.W. Gerberdings' sons were appointed to the management of the company. While Horst took over the perfumery division of Dragoco, his older brother Carl-Heinz devoted himself to expanding the international business. Carl-Heinz Gerberding continued to expand the international business and founded the company's first US division in 1956. In his memoirs, the eldest son of the company founder explains that his motivation was to become independent of Germany by internationalising the company.

In the difficult early days, he had to use tricks and tactics to convince his father, who traditionally saw more potential for success in the domestic business, of the success of the international business. However, the American subsidiary soon grew and became a key part of the international business. Wilhelm-Karl Prince of Prussia also joined the Dragoco management team and took over from Heinrich Haensel.

In 1957, company founder C.W. Gerberding retired owing to health reasons and moved to Switzerland.

These pictures also bear witness to a mood of optimism: the Dragoco branch in Totowa, USA, built in 1960.

1956 – 2002

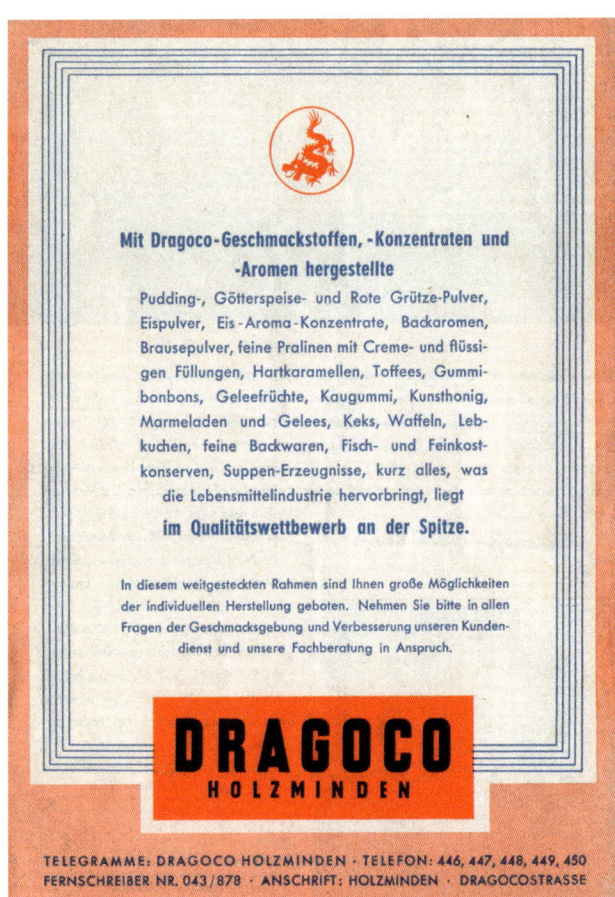

At the end of the 1950s, Dragoco emphasises that it can now offer flavours that are *"better than before the war"*.

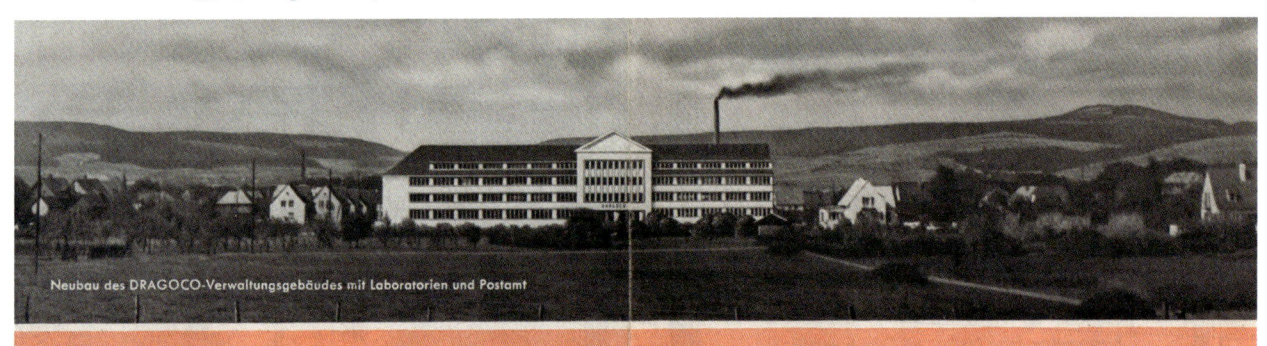

Worldwide Growth

New production facilities were also built on the Haarmann & Reimer site in the late 1950s / early 1960s, while the old buildings were gradually demolished. (photos right and left).

Expansion of the plant facilities at Haarmann & Reimer

Bayer's financial strength enabled Haarmann & Reimer to proceed with the urgently needed modernisation of the plant in Holzminden. Some of the facilities and many of the buildings on the site between Holzminden and Altendorf date back to the 19th century. On the occasion of the official opening of a new production hall, the Holzminden daily newspaper Hannoversche Presse wrote under the headline: *"Topping-out ceremony at Haarmann & Reimer / New development opportunities created / Dye Factory Bayer now sole shareholder / Rumours put right"* that the hall "is intended to increase capacity, rationalisation and modernisation". In his official speech, Managing Director Dr. Grogers emphasised that Haarmann & Reimer had needed additional capital in order to catch up with the development of the foreign companies after the war: *"For understandable reasons, such capital could not come from private funds from the founding families."*

"The former shareholders of Haarmann und Reimer, thus, made it possible to establish contact with the dyestuffs company Farbenfabriken Bayer AG Leverkusen. After the war, Farbenfabriken Bayer took over the Agfa fragrance department, which had been set up at the dyestuffs company Farbenfabriken Wolfen, and incorporated it into its Uerdingen plant. In October 1953, the decision was made to transfer this fragrance business to Haarmann & Reimer and, simultaneously, to acquire shares in the company in order to provide it with the capital required to achieve the company's

1956 – 2002

Visible growth: old and new boiler house, 1959

objectives as outlined above". Dr. Grogers then emphasised that *"the character of Haarmann & Reimer and the purpose of the company have not changed and will not change in any way."*

Significant growth for Haarmann & Reimer between 1952 and 1960

The employment and turnover figures of Haarmann & Reimer for the period 1952 until 1960 show that the numbers of employees had doubled from 260 to 599; turnover had increased six fold from almost DM 5 million to DM 30 million; and the export ratio had doubled from 17% to 33%. The latter was a result of the takeover by Bayer that enabled the company to soon establish subsidiaries in Mexico, the USA, Brazil, Great Britain, France and Spain.

Graphic representation of the development of Haarmann & Reimer's workforce and sales between 1952 and 1960

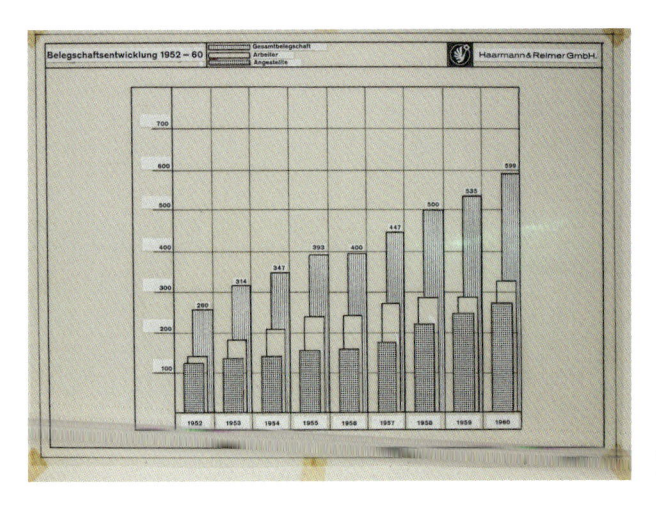

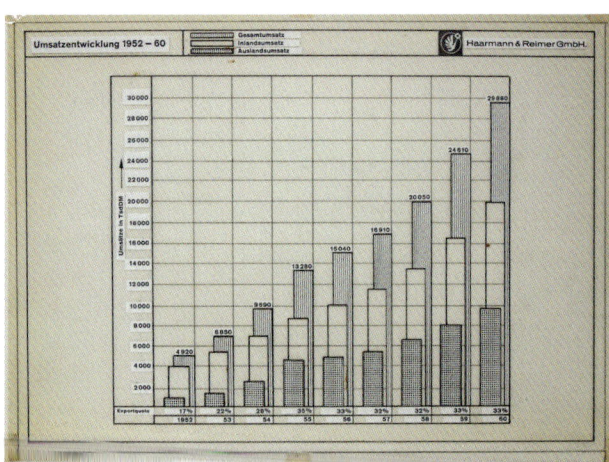

Worldwide Growth

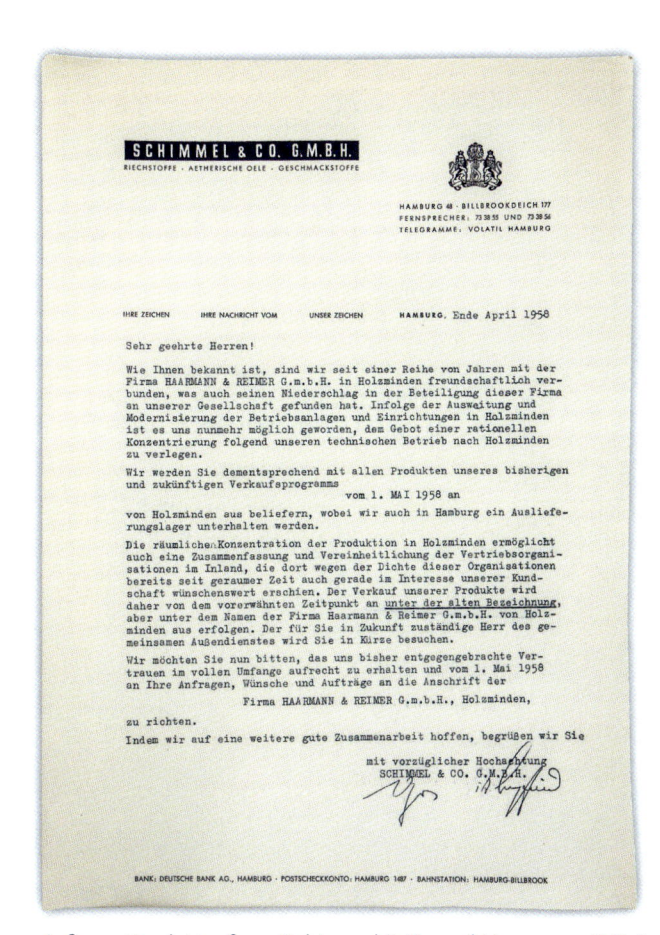

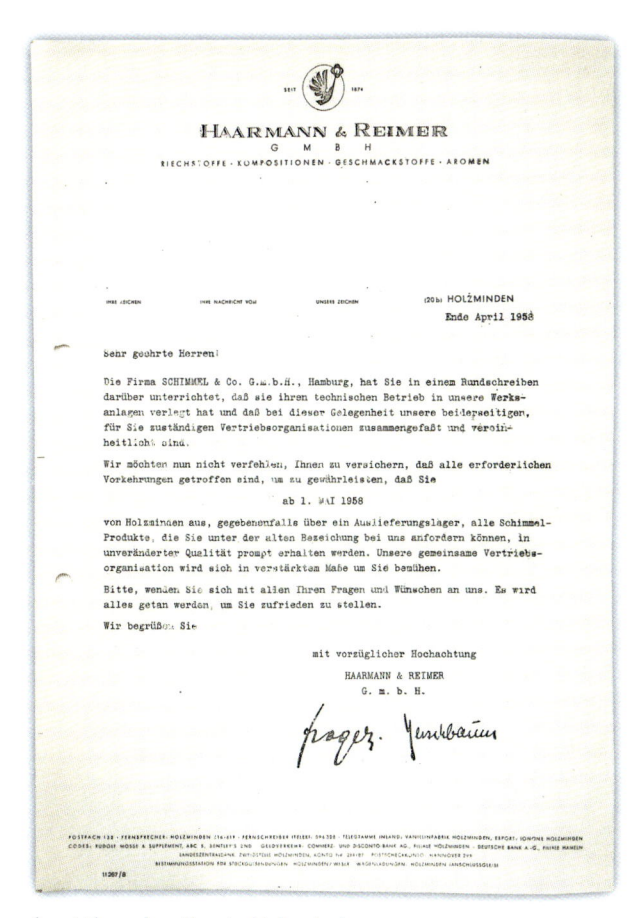

Information letter from Schimmel & Co and Haarmann & Reimer about the relocation to Holzminden

Schimmel & Co is fully integrated into Haarmann & Reimer

At the end of April 1958, Schimmel & Co Hamburg informed its customers: *"As you already know, we have been on friendly terms with Haarmann & Reimer GmbH in Holzminden for a number of years and this has also seen them acquire a stake in our company. As a result of the expansion and modernisation of the production facilities and equipment in Holzminden, it has now become possible for us to relocate our technical operations to Holzminden in line with the need for rational concentration."*

1964 – Dragoco donates research prize

In 1964, Dragoco set up the Otto Wallach Fund at the German Chemical Society in memory of the chemist Otto Wallach as a way of demonstrating its appreciation of research. From 1966 to 2002, the society used these funds to award the Otto Wallach Plaque, which included a cash prize, to researchers from European countries for their special achievements in the field of essential oils, terpenes and polyterpenes or biochemical attractants and deterrents.

The occasion for the establishment of the fund was the 70th birthday of the company founder. The town of Holzminden also took this opportunity to award Carl Wilhelm Gerberding honorary citizenship.

Otto Wallach (* 27 March 1847 in Königsberg i. Pr.; † 26 February 1931 in Göttingen) was a German chemist and Nobel Prize winner. Wallach was an organic chemist and discovered several reactions in the construction of heterocyclic compounds and dyes. Wallach also made fundamental contributions to terpene chemistry, including the structural elucidation and synthesis of this class of substances.

1956 – 2002

Over the years, there have been explosions and fires in the plants of the Holzminden companies. The explosion at Haarmann & Reimer in 1961, in which two workers were injured, resulted in reports in the national press.

Although the Haarmann & Reimer and Dragoco works fire brigades were consolidated following the merger to form Symrise, there are still two locations with emergency vehicles at the Solling and Weser plants. In addition, the works fire brigade has always worked closely with the Holzminden voluntary fire brigade.

Worldwide Growth

In the 1960s, Haarmann & Reimer developed in two directions with the site of the former grinding mill on the corner of Mühlenfeldstrasse and Rumohrtalstrasse being developed with research and administration buildings, and the buildings of 'Schmidtmann's farm' on Altendorfer Strasse being demolished to make way for production and storage buildings.

1968 – More than 1000 employees

In 1968, the number of employees at Haarmann & Reimer exceeded 1,000, having doubled within ten years and, once again, made the company the largest fragrance company in Holzminden. A new research building was built on Rumohrtalstrasse. One year later, a loading facility with a railway siding was built as Haarmann & Reimer shifted shipping from road to rail. Since the Bayer takeover, the site had grown from 70,000 to 220,000 square metres.

In a brochure from that time, Haarmann & Reimer showed current pictures of the factory site as well as photos of historical facilities to document the modernisation of production. The brochure presents all Haarmann & Reimer departments with photos from development and production. A caption on distillation bubbles reads: *"This plant is also part of H&R flavour production. Everything is clear, functional, clean - clean and pure, just like H&R flavours."*

The company's export share was 35%. Dr. Claus Skopalik replaced Dr. Rudolf Grogers on the management board. The acquisition of Esarom GmbH Nördlingen expanded the product range to include beverage bases and additives. The Holzminden-based company Bohnsack & Co GmbH Holzminden, which was founded in 1946 by former Haarmann & Reimer employees, was also taken over. According to former Works Council Chairman Karl-Heinz Huchthausen, Managing Director Skopalik and his deputy Georg Kerschbaum put the company on a steady and successful growth path, from which the company's employees also benefitted greatly.

1968 – Reform of patent law

In the period around 1900, the development of Haarmann & Reimer was strongly characterised by disputes over the patent protection of the products developed. From the point of view of research-oriented companies, this was due to the inadequate regulations in the German Patent Act of 1877, which only protected the manufacturing process for synthesised and artificial substances, not the new chemical compound itself. It was not until 1968 that absolute substance protection was introduced in Germany, modelled on US patent law. This meant that chemical compounds could be patented regardless of their use. Absolute substance protection also extended to possible uses that were not known to the patent holder at the time of application.

Construction work at Dragoco in 1964 (left) and in the 1970s to the east of the main building (right)

Dragoco reports

From the 1950s onwards, with the quarterly publication *DRAGOCO BERICHTE - Marktbericht, Forschungsbericht, Preisbericht* (DRAGOCO REPORTS - Market Report, Research Report, Price Report), the company continued the tradition of the highly regarded reports of Schimmel & Co, at least in terms of name. However, while the Schimmel reports dealt with general scientific topics in the fragrance and flavour industry, the DRAGOCO BERICHTE were devoted more to the company's self-promotion.

The DRAGOCO BERICHTE were published from 1953 to 1997 in A5 format and from the late 1950s, they were supplemented by the dragoco report. The former now specifically addressed the flavour-processing industries, the latter were of a more general nature and tended to cover popular fragrance topics. Both publications were also published in English, Spanish and occasionally Italian.

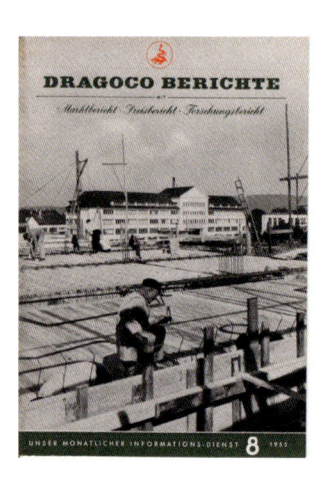

A very early issue of DRAGOCO REPORTS from 1953

On the one hand, the DRAGOCO REPORTS documented the expansion of the plant, and on the other, specialist articles were also published.

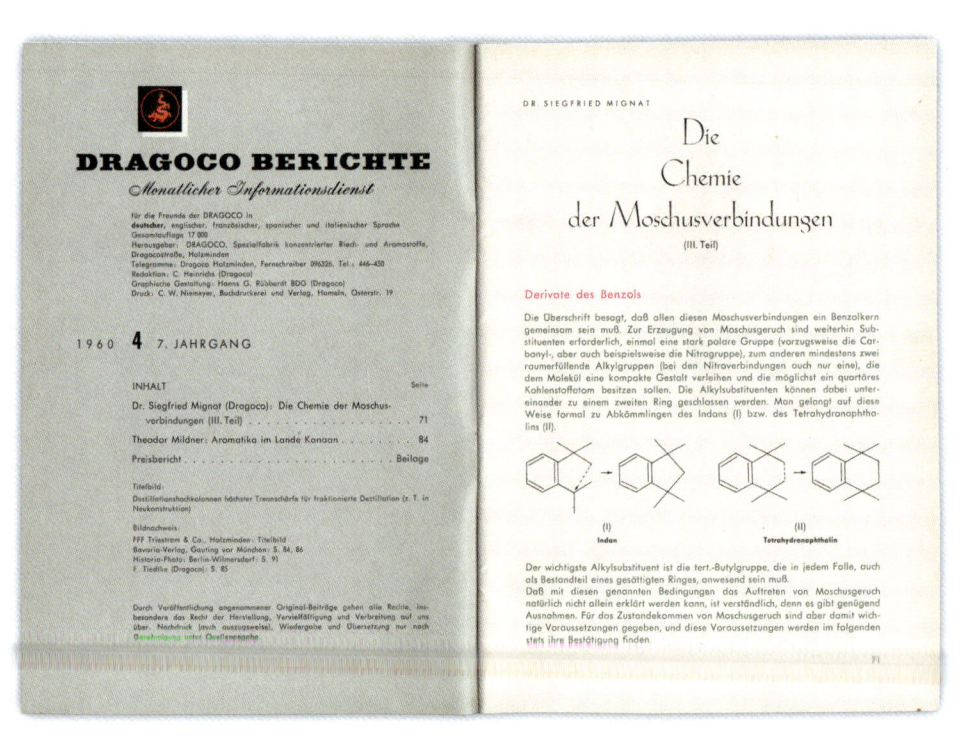

Worldwide Growth

Montag, 27. Oktober 1969

50 Jahre Dragoco

Vom kleinen Labor in der Bahnhofsstraße zum Unternehmen von Weltruf

Vor 50 Jahren begann Carl Wilhelm Gerberding in einem kleinen Labor in der Bahnhofstraße mit der Herstellung von Haarwasser. Mit kaufmännischer Begabung und einem Gespür für diese seltsame Branche entwickelte er aus kleinsten Anfängen eine Firma, die heute Weltgeltung besitzt: die „Dragoco" — Spezialfabrik konzentrierter Riech- und Aromastoffe Gerberding u. Co GmbH in Holzminden. 300 maßgebliche Unternehmen dieser Branche gibt es in der Welt, etwa 15 mischen entscheidend auf dem Weltmarkt mit und unter diesen steht — neben Haarmann und Reimer, Holzminden — heute die Dragoco. Das wurde anläßlich des Jubiläums, das am Wochenende begangen wurde, mit berechtigtem Stolz festgestellt.

Die Dragoco, das ist nicht nur das stark expandierende Werk mit 650 Beschäftigten und der Hauptverwaltung in Holzminden. Zur Firmengruppe, die sich im Jubiläumsjahr der 100-Millionen-Umsatzgrenze nähert und 1000 Menschen beschäftigt, gehören auch Schwestern- bzw. Tochtergesellschaften in Großbritannien, Frankreich, Österreich, Italien, USA und Mexico und Verkaufsbüros in der Schweiz, in Spanien, Japan und Australien. Die Firma, die in den letzten fünf Jahren 25 Millionen Mark investierte — allein die jetzt in Holzminden zusätzlich erstellten Hallen stehen mit fünf Millionen zu Buche — beabsichtigt in naher Zukunft auch in Südostasien stärker Fuß zu fassen und außerdem den südamerikanischen Markt zu erobern.

Das von Carl Wilhelm Gerberding, der an seinem 70. Geburtstag zum Ehrenbürger Holzminden ernannt wurde, gegründete Unternehmen ist ein reines Familienunternehmen. Inhaber sind heute die beiden Söhne des Gründers, Geschäftsführer in Holzminden sind Carl Heinz Gerberding und Wilhelm Karl Prinz von Preußen.

Die Besitzer sehen auch für die Zukunft die Chance, als Familienunternehmen neben Großkonzernen zu bestehen. Sie wenden sich daher bewußt von der Herstellung konventioneller Riechstoffe ab und forcieren die Spezialisierung, die ihnen eine Sonderstellung und — die Zukunft zu sichern verspricht. Die Stärke des Unternehmens liegt in der engen Zusammenarbeit mit den Abnehmern der Erzeugnisse. Dragoco ist ausschließlich Zulieferer und will seinen Abnehmern keinesfalls mit eigenen Fertigprodukten Konkurrenz machen.

Jubiläumsveranstaltung in neuer Halle

In der neuen Produktionshalle, aus der die Bauunternehmer gerade ausgezogen, die Maschinen aber noch nicht eingezogen waren, feierte das Unternehmen jetzt mit seiner gesamten Belegschaft das 50jährige Bestehen. Wilhelm Karl Prinz von Preußen schilderte den Werdegang der Dragoco, umriß ihre heutige Stellung und sprach namens der Inhaber und der Geschäftsleitung den Dank an alle Mitarbeiter aus. Jubiläumsgeschenk an alle Dragoco-Mitarbeiter ist eine neu eingerichtete Pensionskasse, auf deren Leistungen alle Betriebsangehörigen nach einer bestimmten Dauer der Betriebszugehörigkeit einen Anspruch haben.

Ihren Dank an Stadt und Landkreis stattet die Firma mit einem „namhaften" Betrag zur Modernisierung des evangelischen Krankenhauses in Holzminden ab.

Bürgermeister Willi Wolf würdigte in der Feierstunde die Verdienste Carl Wilhelm Gerberdings, dessen unternehmerischer Geist dazu beitrug, ein Werk zu schaffen, das heute vielen Holzmindenern eine berufliche Heimat bietet. Wolf dankte für eine vertrauensvolle und gute Zusammenarbeit. Mit einem Geschenk, das man für Geld nicht kaufen kann — eine Holzmindener Notgeldsammlung — gratulierte die Stadt dem Jubiläumsbetrieb.

Der Präsident der Bundesvereinigung Deutscher Arbeitgeberverbände, Prof. Dr. Siegfried Balke, hielt das Jubiläumsreferat über Zukunftsaufgaben für Staat und Wirtschaft. Balke kam zu der Überzeugung, daß der selbständige Unternehmer auch in der von kollektiver Verantwortung geprägten Umwelt eine Aufgabe habe. Das Leistungsprinzip müsse nach seiner Ansicht auch in dem Wirtschaftsgefüge der Zukunft Vorrang vor dem Anspruchsprinzip haben.

Prince Wilhelm Karl of Prussia during his speech at Dragoco's 50th anniversary celebration

IN DER ERSTEN REIHE bei der Jubiläumsveranstaltung in der neuen, noch maschinenleeren Produktionshalle der Dragoco, Firmengründer Carl Wilhelm Gerberding mit Gattin und den Söhnen, den heutigen Hauptgesellschaftern des Unternehmens.

Twenty-five years after the end of the war, Dragoco celebrated its 50th anniversary. Almost symbolically for the company's further growth, the guests were invited to the newly completed building. Above is the Hannoversche Presse report on the event. The Holzminden-based Täglicher Anzeiger newspaper reported that the company had expanded its production programme considerably, particularly since the Second World War: *"The slogan 'The scent that accompanies a beautiful woman is prepared in Holzminden' is true, but it does not do justice to the importance of Holzminden's fragrance and flavour industry, or Dragoco. The programme is much more comprehensive."*

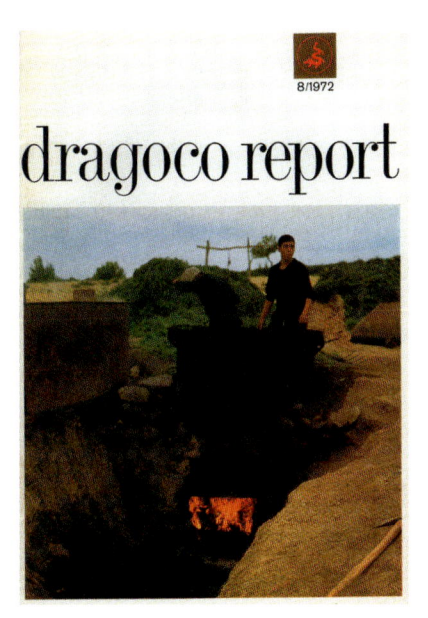

The dragoco report from August 1972 describes how rosemary oil is distilled in the fields in Tunisia.

1969: aerial photos of Haarmann & Reimer (above) and Dragoco (below)

Worldwide Growth

1970 – Marketing with H&R Contact

Haarmann & Reimer launched the *H&R Contact* magazine, a long-term marketing measure in the form of an attractive magazine in A4 format. The publication was not intended for the general public, but its contemporary design and wide range of topics appealed to a large number of people in the fragrance and flavour industry. The magazine not only covered news from the company and industry-specific topics, the '*H&R Contact visits customers*' series also revealed which brands were supplied by Haarmann & Reimer. *H&R Contact* was published in German and English.

International studios for customer service

The Holzminden location offers both advantages and disadvantages for a branch of industry that tends to work in the background because, on the one hand, no end products are created there and, on the other, customers do not attach any great importance to naming suppliers. For one, the rural seclusion allows the company to concentrate fully on the development and production of fragrances and flavourings. However, in the last third of the 20th century, the demands of customers in the business-to-business sector also increased and the buyers of major brand manufacturers wanted to be treated appropriately. Be that as it may, most of the foreign branches of the Holzminden-based fragrance and flavouring companies are purely production facilities and sales offices. In the 1970s, Haarmann & Reimer, therefore, began to set up representative studios. A perfume studio was set up in Cannes and the branch in the World Trade Center in New York was a prime address from the late 1970s onwards. Haarmann & Reimer had already moved into another office in New York City in the 1990s. Dragoco set up a branch in Grasse, France in 1974 to present new developments in the field of perfume compositions.

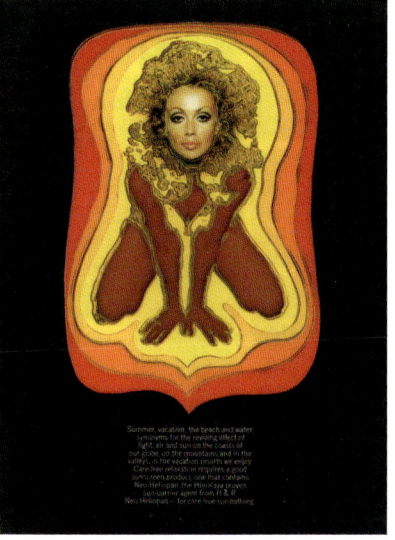

The magazine H&R Contact was published from 1970 (top right); in 1979 it reported on the studio in the World Trade Center.

1956 – 2002

Aerial view of the Dragoco factory premises from the 1970s

The aerial photograph of Haarmann & Reimer dates from the same period. A number of new buildings were constructed at the end of the 1960s / beginning of the 1970s, particularly south of Rumohrtalstrasse.

1973 – Expansion of the Dragoco factory site
Worldwide subsidiaries

In 1973, the factory premises in Holzminden continued to expand with the construction of a technical application centre for fragrances and compositions, and a building for the works fire brigade. However, the internationalisation of the company also continued. With the help of independent employees, Dragoco subsidiaries were founded in Europe, America, Australia and Asia. At the same time, the production facilities in the USA were expanded.

1973 – Haarmann & Reimer development of fully synthetic menthol

In 1973, Haarmann & Reimer succeeded in producing fully synthetic menthol, the main component of peppermint oil, for the first time. The substance corresponded to natural menthol and was, therefore, considered 'nature-identical'. Dragoco had expanded its production on a large scale in the 1950s. One third of the world's production volume was now synthetic. Menthol is used as a fragrance and flavouring agent, but also as a disinfectant ingredient in ointments and other personal care products. It was not until 1984 that a second manufacturer of synthetic menthol, the Japanese company Takasago, entered the market. Today, menthol is also produced by BASF (since 2012). The use of menthol in the flavouring of tobacco is controversial, as menthol reduces the sensation of irritation and pain when inhaling the smoke.

Holzminden builds wastewater treatment plant for 400,000 inhabitants

In May 1974, the local newspaper, Tägliche Anzeiger reported on the construction of a new wastewater treatment plant for Holzminden. The fully biological plant was designed for "*the equivalent of 400,000 inhabitants*". The report states: "*The town council is working on the basis that Holzminden is one of the places in northern Germany with the most difficult wastewater to treat. It is now certain that almost 75 per cent of the wastewater to be treated in Holzminden comes from the large chemical plants. The city has been in negotiations with them for six months. The question is whether or not these industries can feed pre-treated wastewater into the new biological treatment plant on Nordstrasse.*" The article states that a trial operation was planned. The difficulties in treating the wastewater could "*at best be comparable to those in Leverkusen and Dormagen*". It goes on to say: "Holzminden, which has long been urged by higher authorities to build a biological sewage treatment plant, wants to make an important contribution to a cleaner Weser."

Older files show that Haarmann & Reimer had installed a wastewater pipe with direct access to the Weser in the early days. It was not connected to the Holzminden sewerage system until the 1930s. However, wastewater was also discharged into the Holzminden streams, which converged on the company premises, and this sometimes had fatal consequences for life in the stream as evidenced by a press report from 6 August 1955 about fish dying in the Herrenbach stream below the chemical works.

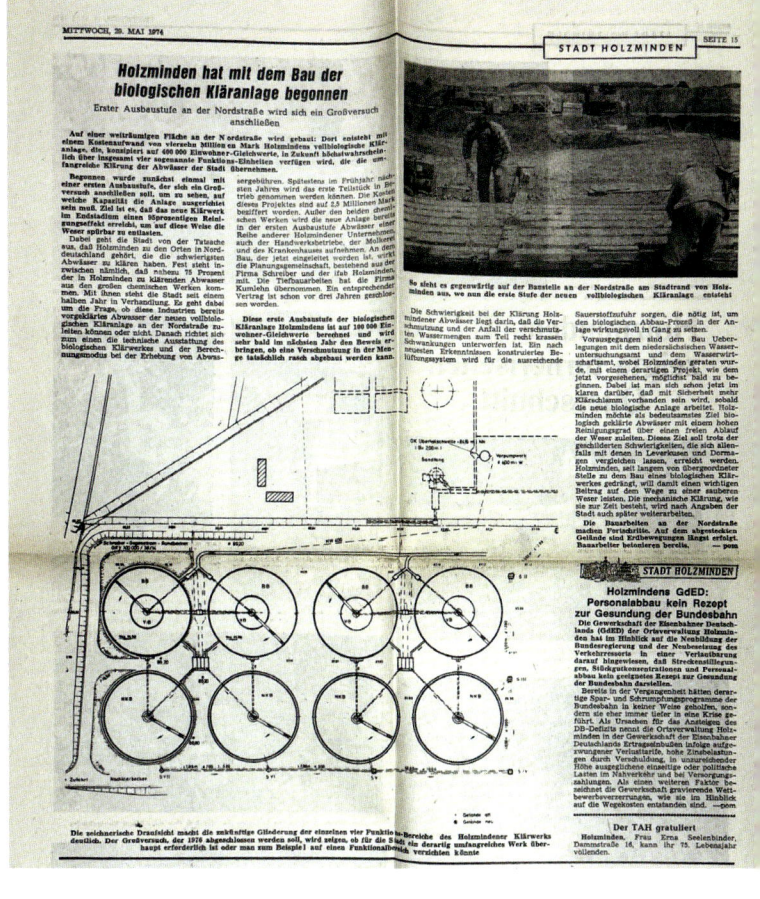

Newspaper reports on the new sewage treatment plant (1974) and the death of fish in the Herrenbache (1955)

1956 – 2002

Natural, artificial, synthetic

Changes in the use of language and defintions

Paulina S. Gennermann wrote in her book A History with Taste: *"The 1960s focused on two primary fields of action for companies in the flavour and fragrance industry: firstly, they had to actively participate in the emerging European regulation and, secondly, they had to counteract the negativity of the terms 'synthetic' and 'artificial' in this context."*

In principle, little has changed in this respect for flavour and fragrance companies: On the one hand, industrial food production by large corporations requires consistent quality and punctual delivery of additives, while, on the other hand, the multitude of new technical, biotechnological and genetic engineering production processes continue to cause consumers to fear synthetic additives - they want sustainably produced natural food. Regulation (EC) No. 1334/2008 lays down uniform rules throughout Europe that only authorised flavouring substances may be sold and processed in foodstuffs. The regulation specifies which flavourings must be evaluated and approved and those which do not need to be evaluated or approved. Flavourings may only be used if they do not pose a risk to consumers and do not mislead them. Since the EU Flavourings Regulation came into force in 2009, a distinction is no longer made between 'natural', 'nature-identical' and 'artificial' flavourings. The terms 'nature-identical' and 'artificial' have been deleted; both types of flavourings now fall under the general term 'flavouring'. According to this regulation, a distinction is essentially made between the two categories 'natural flavourings' and 'flavourings'.

All chemically defined substances with flavouring properties can be described as flavourings. A so-called 'natural flavouring', on the other hand, is subject to clearly defined requirements regarding its origin or production. This term may only be used if the substance is obtained by appropriate physical, enzymatic or microbiological processes from vegetable, animal or microbiological base materials which are used as such or which have been prepared for human consumption by one or more specifically defined conventional food preparation processes. Natural flavourings must also occur naturally and have been proven to exist in nature.

In addition to the regulation, the EU provides a constantly updated list of all approved flavourings. It currently lists around 2,500 flavourings which have a unique identification number.

In the 1970s, consumer sensitivity to artificially produced foods was often significantly less pronounced than nowadays: milk drinks from a spray can, as advertised in H&R Contact at the time, seem strange today.

A fragrance organ at Haarmann & Reimer, 1970s

1974 – 100 years Haarmann & Reimer

The company published an elaborately designed book for Haarmann & Reimer's 100th anniversary. It focuses on nature as a supplier of raw materials and role model for the production of synthetic products in the flavour industry: *"The importance of nature as a role model for synthesis was first apparent in the artificial synthesis of vanillin. The culmination of 100 years of development in this field is the industrial scale production of synthetic l-menthol by Haarmann & Reimer. This has made it possible to synthetically, but nature-identically, produce a further indispensable fragrance and flavouring which cannot be supplied in sufficient quantities by nature."* It continues on the topic of the future of flavour production: *"An increasing population and, therefore, an increased demand in foodstuffs are forcing the development of new, high quality forms of food such as protein which is based on seaweed. This goes hand in hand with the development of new flavourings that are tailored to the requirements of highly industrialised food production."*

In addition to a brief outline of the history, the book focuses on the various production areas and Haarmann & Reimer products. For instance, you can read about perfume: *"A fine perfume, composed of exquisite essential oils and synthetic components is a work of art. It is no coincidence that we speak of a fragrance composition and praise the harmony of a fragrance chord. Achieving such harmony depends on the fine tuning of the individual components to each other. The artist whose field of activity is the keyboard*

The Haarmann & Reimer administration building erected in the early 1970s

1956 – 2002

of the perfumer's organ, in other words, the perfumer, describes and organises the world of fragrances which seems almost overwhelming. An excellent sense of smell is his most important tool in doing so. However, his profession also requires him to think rationally, as well as have an understanding of aesthetics and a creative talent. A century ago, 120 to 150 natural fragrances were known. Today, their number, together with fragrances from the retort, is already innumerable."

An article in the local newspaper on 8 October 1974 about the press conference on the 100th anniversary reported: *"The anniversary has been taken as an opportunity to point out that the company does not intend on expanding any further in the town and wants to do even more to protect the environment in the future."*

Dr. Claus Skopalik and lawyer Georg Kerschbaum from the management team described the employment situation as good and the profit situation as satisfactory. Turnover totalled DM 138.2 million with an export share of 42% and a significant increase of both was expected for 1974. The article continued: *"Haarmann & Reimer identifies menthol as the largest source of turnover. Menthol production was started in Holzminden just over a year ago. There are plans to construct a similar plant in the United States, […] to initially cover the American market and later, from there, to cover the global market."* In 1973, the products of head office were being shipped to 112 countries.

Dr. Claus Skopalik

Newspaper report on the centenary of Haarmann & Reimer

Worldwide Growth

Menthol — die kühlenden Kristalle

Das aus dem ätherischen Öl der Pfefferminzpflanze gewonnene natürliche Menthol war das Vorbild für die Entwicklung seines Ebenbildes, l-Menthol H&R. Haarmann & Reimer ist es nach langjähriger Forschungsarbeit gelungen, ein Verfahren zur Herstellung von vollsynthetischem l-Menthol im großtechnischen Maßstab zu entwickeln.
Dieses Spitzenprodukt aus der Retorte der Chemie entspricht in seinen chemischen Konstanten und organoleptischen Eigenschaften dem natürlichen Vorbild so vollkommen, daß es als natur-identisch bezeichnet werden kann. Es kann unabhängig von der Natur in stets gleichbleibender Qualität hergestellt werden. Zwei bedeutende Meilensteine aus einer Vielzahl von Produkten:
1874 synthetisches Vanillin,
1974 synthetisches Menthol: l-Menthol H&R.

Double-page spread from issue 10/1979 of the dragoco report on the occasion of Dragoco's 60th anniversary

Glanzlicht Großfabrikation

In Mono- und Mehrzweckanlagen von imponierenden Dimensionen werden unter Einsatz von Meß- und Regeltechnik einheitliche Riechstoffe von höchster Qualität produziert.
Der weltweit steigende Verbrauch von Parfümölen ist nur vor dem Hintergrund solcher Großanlagen denkbar. So „technisch" sie auch aussehen mögen: sie sind heute das Rückgrat jeglicher kreativer Arbeit des Parfümeurs, denn dessen Kunst besteht nicht zuletzt darin, seine Ideen optimal in individuelle Parfümöle unter Verwendung von preisgünstigen Bausteinen umzusetzen.
Dies ist ihm umso leichter möglich, je reichhaltiger das Angebot an Riechstoffen aus der Großfabrikation ist, ohne die ein marktgerechtes Angebot guter Düfte heute kaum möglich wäre.

1956 – 2002

Specialist newspaper report on Dr Skopalik's 25th anniversary at Bayer and Haarmann & Reimer

Haarmann & Reimer research department, 1974

Slower growth after the 'economic miracle'

In a presentation on the "*long-term corporate concept*" at a flavorist conference in 1976, Dr. Skopalik explained that "*the great backlog of demand for consumer goods that existed after the Second World War, particularly in Europe and Japan, [...] has now been fully met. The production factors of energy, raw materials and, especially, labour have become extremely expensive in the aforementioned regions. There are currently no revolutionary new technologies on the horizon to stimulate growth. For all of the above reasons, production in most industrialised countries will increase far more slowly than the average of the past two decades, at least in the next few years. Global economic growth is predicted to continue, but will shift in particular to resource-rich developing countries.*" The aim of future investments was to be rationalisation rather than capacity expansion. Skopalik now saw the opportunity for general economic growth more in technological progress. According to Skopalik, things were not looking so bad for his own industry, as there was still growing demand in the perfume sector in the "*populous developing countries*".

And when it came to flavourings, "*growth is likely to continue unabated in both industrialised and developing countries.*" The Haarmann & Reimer managing director saw particular growth impulses in the substitution of expensive natural substances with synthetic products, new areas of application for flavourings such as the "*flavouring of semi-synthetic and later synthetic proteins*" and, thirdly, in the "*progressive spread of prefabricated foods (convenience food), which lose flavour during production and, therefore, still need to be flavoured. After all, population growth and an, albeit modest, improvement in living standards in developing countries must lead to a considerable increase in demand for flavourings. All in all, our industry should continue to be among the growth sectors.*" After the recession year of 1975, Skopalik was expecting a further increase in turnover for 1976.

Skopalik saw both peppermint and protein flavourings as future key areas for the flavours division.

Worldwide Growth

Produktion

Wenn es um eine Entscheidung über Zentralisation oder Dezentralisation der Produktion geht, müssen Vor- und Nachteile der Alternativen auch stets aus der Sicht der Kunden in Betracht gezogen werden. Dezentralisierung bedeutet kürzere Lieferzeiten, mehr Flexibilität, Zentralisation dagegen bessere Wirtschaftlichkeit durch größere Ansätze und daher günstigere Preise. Wo hohe Importbarrieren vorliegen, wird eine Produktion im Lande unumgänglich.

Die diesbezüglichen Überlegungen bei DRAGOCO sind flexibel und differenziert: Zentralisation wo möglich, Dezentralisation wo nötig. Parfumkompositionen werden von einer Reihe von DRAGOCO-Gesellschaften produziert. Die Synthese der DRAGOCO-Riechstoff-Spezialitäten, die sehr viel aufwendiger, komplexer und kapitalintensiver ist, liegt z. Z. noch ausschließlich beim Stammhaus Holzminden. Die kosmetischen Wirkstoffe werden zum großen Teil in Holzminden angefertigt. Bestimmte Spezialitäten werden jedoch auch an anderen Stellen produziert, so z. B. eine Reihe von Pflanzendestillaten und -extrakten von DRAGOCO Wien.

In einer Produktionshalle der Dragoco Österreich. Links eine Reihe von Lagergefäßen für die Herstellung von Pflanzenextrakten. Eine längere Lagerung ist hier erforderlich, um zu gewährleisten, daß bei dem fertigen, filtrierten Extrakt keine Nachtrübungen auftreten.

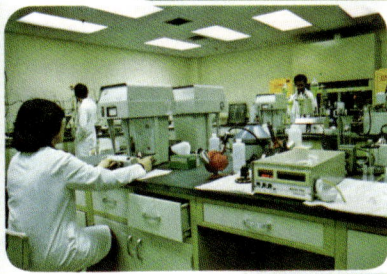

Die Produktions-Abteilung der Dragoco Brasilien, São Paulo, arbeitet regelmäßig in mehreren Schichten. Die ersten Schritte zum Bau einer neuen größeren Produktionsanlage wurden bereits unternommen.

Bei der Produktions-Qualitätskontrolle von Parfumkompositionen unterliegt jedes Parfum einer doppelten Prüfung: der chemisch-analytischen und der sensorischen, d. h. dem Geruchstest. Links oben Blick in das Laboratorium für Qualitätskontrolle der Dragoco Totowa, rechts das Qualitätskontroll-Panel der Dragoco Holzminden bei der Arbeit.

Blick in eine Produktionshalle der Dragoco Mexico. In Ländern mit Importbeschränkungen ist eine Eigenproduktion unumgänglich.

258

Double-page spread from issue 10/1979 of the dragoco report on the occasion of Dragoco's 60th anniversary

Kreative Parfümerie

Diese war schon immer und ist auch heute noch das Herz eines jeden Hauses, das Parfumkompositionen entwickelt. Auch der Erfolg unseres Hauses hängt vor allem anderen davon ab, daß unsere Parfümeure Parfums kreieren, die dem Geschmack des Publikums und den Qualitätsansprüchen des Kunden entsprechen, die allen technischen Anforderungen in bezug auf Duft, Farbbeständigkeit, Löslichkeit, Haftung usw. gerecht werden und die den immer strenger werdenden gesetzlichen Verordnungen und spezifischen Firmenwünschen hinsichtlich Hautverträglichkeit und gesundheitlicher Unbedenklichkeit Rechnung tragen.

Diese zentrale Stellung des Parfümeurs ist allerdings einer der wenigen Aspekte seiner Arbeit, der sich in den letzten Jahren nicht grundlegend geändert hat. Mit einigen der vielen Änderungen wollen wir uns auf den folgenden Seiten dieses Dragoco Report befassen. Zunächst wollen wir aber nur auf einen besonders wichtigen Aspekt in diesem Zusammenhang eingehen.

Man denkt oft noch an den Parfümeur als alleinschaffenden Künstler. Dieses Bild hat nie so ganz den Tatsachen entsprochen, doch trifft es heute weniger denn je zuvor zu. Die Schöpfung eines Parfums wird immer mehr zur Teamarbeit. So verwendet ein Parfümeur bei der Entwicklung einer

Gene Morgan, Vizepräsident der Fragrance Division, Dragoco Totowa, New Jersey (USA), ist ein überzeugter Verfechter der EDV als Arbeitshilfsmittel des Parfümeurs. Neben seinen administrativen Aufgaben findet Mr. Morgan immer noch Zeit zu kreativer Arbeit an wichtigen Projekten.

Ralf Knollmann, Chefparfümeur in Holzminden, an seinem Arbeitsplatz. Mit seinen über 20 Jahren Berufserfahrung ist Ralf Knollmann, neben seiner kreativen Arbeit an allen wichtigen Projekten, Lehrer der jüngeren Parfümeure und ein hochgeschätzter Berater unserer Kunden.

Die Laboratorien des internationalen Parfümerie-Zentrums der Dragoco Paris liegen, knapp 2 km vom Arc de Triomphe entfernt, im Stadtteil Neuilly. Hier einer der Senior-Parfümeure, André Girodroux, im Gespräch mit einer Assistentin.

237

Photo of the production facilities at Dragoco, which was published in an illustrated book about the town of Holzminden, with the caption: '*With the high concentration of fragrances and flavourings, the contents of one container are enough to perfume around 8 million bars of soap or flavour around 50 million 250-g bags of sweets, for example.*'

1977 – More than 1,000 employees at Dragoco

In 1977, the number of employees at Dragoco reached 1,000, meaning that the two Holzminden-based fragrance and flavour companies together had more than 2,000 employees, the majority of whom worked in Holzminden. In the early years after the Second World War, Stiebel Eltron and some companies in the wood processing industry were the most important employers in the Weser town, but this changed in the 1970s. Today, the chemical industry is still the most important employer in the region.

1981 – Horst-Otto Gerberding became managing director of Dragoco GmbH

Horst-Otto Gerberding, the son of Carl-Heinz Gerberding, joined the management of Dragoco Holzminden in 1981, representing the 3rd generation of the Gerberding family. The company's international growth to date had been based on the concept of placing largely independent subsidiaries in the hands of proven employees. From the 1980s onwards, the subsidiaries were more closely integrated into the globally active company.

Horst-Otto Gerberding at the anniversary of the Dragoco works fire brigade in 1989. The fire brigade had been founded 40 years earlier. A devastating fire in a warehouse near the Stiebel Eltron plant also destroyed valuable raw materials belonging to Dragoco. In view of the extent of the damage, the management decided to set up a works fire brigade, which has been continuously updated and improved ever since.

1984 – Haarmann & Reimer fragrance atlases

In co-operation with Glöss Verlag Hamburg, Haarmann & Reimer had been publishing four large-format and comprehensive fragrance atlases since 1984. The Haarmann & Reimer book Parfum (Perfume) deals with the history, origin, development and significance

Worldwide Growth

of perfume scents. The atlases on feminine and masculine notes, H&R Duftatlas Damen-Noten and H&R Duftatlas Herren-Noten, provide an overview of the classification of fragrances according to fragrance families and present current fragrances with illustrations of the original bottles and descriptions of top, heart and base notes. The H&R Lexicon of Fragrance Components defines *"341 fragrance components of natural and synthetic origin according to origin, extraction, form, yield, use and fragrance"*. The processes for extracting the fragrances are also described in detail and graphically illustrated in the encyclopaedia.

Haarmann & Reimer started menthol production in the USA in 1978 with the opening of the Bushy Park production facility in South Carolina. The Bayer Group invested 100 million dollars in the construction of this plant. Five years earlier, Haarmann & Reimer had developed the process and used it in production for the first time in Holzminden.

With the H&R Fragrance Atlases, the company published standard works that still attract attention today.

1956 – 2002

DRAGOCO

Carl Wilhelm Gerberding 1894–1984

In memory and in honour of the company founder, Dragoco published a brochure on the life and work of Carl Wilhelm Gerberding in the style of the dragoco report.

1984 – Carl Wilhelm Gerberding dies

A special edition of the Dragoco Report was published in honour of Carl Wilhelm Gerberding's life's work. Prince Wilhelm Karl of Prussia wrote about him in the article 'Looking back and ahead': *"Until the very end, Carl Wilhelm Gerberding followed his life's work – 'his child DRAGOCO', as he liked to say – with great interest and tried to give some advice from his wealth of experience. He was never a man who took the easy way for himself or for anyone else. That's probably always the case with founding fathers. But he was a great benefactor to many, providing them with work, bread and a new home in difficult times. It was out of nothing that he built an exemplary family business, which in the following generations carried his and the name of his hometown around the world and today has international recognition. Of course, Carl Wilhelm Gerberding was also lucky. But, according to Moltke, it was the kind of luck that only the diligent will have in the long run. [...] He proved his courage and willpower as a young war holidaymaker when he saved a child, who had fallen through the ice, from drowning. He always considered the Lifesaving Medal, which he received at the time, to be his most important award. [...]*

It was a full life, and according to the old Bible verse, it must have been precious to him, precisely because it took effort and hard work. If he has now returned to his native Weserbergland in his 10th decade of life, one could say of him, as of Job in the Bible: 'He died old and satisfied with life' because he consciously experienced his DRAGOCO in the year of its greatest heyday and because he saw the continued existence of his family as secured."

1989 – Establishment and expansion of Dragoco regional centres

In the same year, Dragoco Hong Kong relocated to Singapore. DM 27 million was invested in the establishment and expansion of this company. Singapore became

Aerial view of the Dragoco factory premises from the 1990s

Worldwide Growth

the new regional centre for Asia alongside the regional centres in New York for America, Sao Paulo for South America and Holzminden for Europe. Dragoco Vienna had already been responsible for the Comecon countries since the 1970s. In the 1990s, it was also assigned responsibility for the Middle East and South Africa for perfumery and cosmetics.

1993 – Restructuring of the Dragoco Group
The retirement of shareholder Horst F.W. Gerberding made it necessary to reorganise the Dragoco Group. The holding companies of Dragoco Switzerland with subsidiaries in Asia and Dragoco Inc. USA were merged with Dragoco GmbH in Holzminden. The GmbH (private limited company) was subsequently converted into an AG (public limited company). Equita (Harald Quandt) acquired a 25.1 % stake in this public limited company. The aim of this new structure was a flotation on the stock market. In order to maintain the high investment volume, the Nord LB bank acquired a stake in the company as a preference shareholder. A sum of over DM 100 million was invested in Holzminden alone in the 1990s. It started with the new flavour development. The modernisation of the plant continued with an automatic production line for liquid flavours and perfume oils, a new spray tower for flavours and the complete renewal of the chemical production including storage for special substances.

The Management Board was made up of
Horst-Otto Gerberding - Chairman of the Board
Dietrich Fuhrmann
Richard Winter - CFO

Later, the regional structure with its four regional centres was abandoned in favour of a divisional organisation with a uniform IT platform.

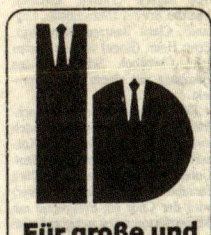

In 1987, Carl-Heinz Gerberding retired. His son Horst-Otto Gerberding and Dietrich Fuhrmann took over overall responsibility for the international side of the business. The photograph shows the senior partner in 1997 with Holzminden's mayor Uwe Schünemann awarding him honorary citizenship.

In 1995, the press can report on an economically successful anniversary year 1994 at Dragoco.

1956 – 2002

Haarmann und Reimer bought the site of the former timber saccharification plant in 1988. The bright red barrel warehouse can already be seen on the right-hand edge of the aerial photograph.

New construction at Haarmann & Reimer on Mühlenfeldstrasse, 1993

1990 – Haarmann & Reimer took over major fragrance and flavour manufacturer

In 1990, Haarmann & Reimer took over the fragrance manufacturer Création Aromatiques and, in 1992, the perfumery business of PFW. In 1993, Haarmann & Reimer generated a group turnover of DM 1.3 billion (€ 651.4 million). Lambert Courth became the new managing director and Dr. Reinhard Kaiser his deputy.

On its 120th anniversary in 1994, Haarmann & Reimer had 30 companies worldwide and representatives in 97 countries. The company ensured standardised production with DQS certification in accordance with DIN ISO 9001/9002. With a turnover of DM 1.4 billion in 1994, Haarmann & Reimer had 4,500 employees worldwide, 1,200 of them in Holzminden. One year later, Bayer took over the flavourings manufacturer Florasynth from the USA with 900 employees worldwide and integrated it into Haarmann & Reimer's business. The Haarmann & Reimer Group turnover, thus, grew to around DM 1.75 billion. Due to the highly competitive market, the importance of vanillin production at Haarmann & Reimer declined significantly in the 20th century. However, the topic

Worldwide Growth

In 1996, two streets in Holzminden were closed to the public: Rumohrtalstrasse, formerly Fabrikstrasse, was turned back into a factory street because the premises of Haarmann & Reimer had since expanded on both sides of the street, so closing it to through traffic was simply a matter of course. It was a similar situation at Kokenhammer, where only pedestrians and cyclists had recently still been permitted to cross the Dragoco premises anyway. After the post office closed, there was no longer any public use of this area either.

of vanillin was never completely dropped, which is why the company was able to register a patent for the biotechnological production of vanillin in the 1990s. The vanillin produced from eugenol in this process is considered a natural flavouring.

Dragoco's turnover is 'not looking rosy'

A report in the *Welt* on 21.07.1999 about Dragoco's newly established Hamburg competence centre stated that the Group had been restructured at an investment cost of around 66 million marks in order to be equipped for the global market. "*As a result, the balance sheet figures did not look rosy. The result from ordinary business operations fell from 36.2 million marks in the previous year to 16 million marks. The Group's result shows a deficit of 2.5 million marks (previous year: plus 16.8 million marks).*" Horst-Otto Gerberding is quoted as saying: "*We are not satisfied with the result.*" However, he was expecting a consolidated net profit of 12.4 million marks that year and moderate growth of five per cent. "*For the year 2000, we are counting on a turnover boost from investments.*" The newspaper report continues: "*Dragoco is opening a creative studio in New York for its fine fragrance business in order to keep its finger on the pulse in America. [...] In the medium term, the management board wants Dragoco to become a public company. The two banks Nord LB and Deutsche Bank are available as syndicate leaders.*" Gerberding: "*Our goal is to go on the official market, but not yet in this year.*"

However, the goal of a flotation on the public market was not pursued any further. In 2000, Dragoco built a new plant in Shanghai, China. At the turn of the century,

Cover page of the Dragoco Report in 1999, the year of the company's 80th anniversary

the company had a total of 25 subsidiaries worldwide and 2,000 employees, of which approximately 800 were in Holzminden. With a turnover of approximately DM 700 million, the export share was approximately 80%.

2000 – successful development of Dragoco
Public offering is not pursued

From the Dragoco Group's perspective, 2000 was a successful year. Consolidated sales increased by 11% to DM 687 million. Despite higher depreciation and interest, the result from ordinary business activities rose by DM 10.6 million to DM 32.8 million. EBITDA totalled DM 88.4 million, the highest result in Dragoco's history. Investments in the 2000 financial year totalled DM 39 million, with an equity ratio of 36.3 %. One of the primary objectives of the planned public offering was to strengthen Dragoco's equity base in order to finance investments on a global scale. Since Dragoco had invested 464 million DM in the 1990s, this target was achieved through its own resources. Future investments were planned at the level of depreciation. Dragoco had a healthy capital structure. A further increase in the equity ratio to 40% was planned. Givaudan had also successfully gone public, which meant that both the number one and two players in the industry, Givaudan and IFF - International Flavors & Fragrances, were already listed on the stock exchange and would have made the planned floatation for Dragoco, number seven in the industry, very difficult.

Dragoco subsidiary in Shanghai

The 20th century also marked the end of security

The two Holzminden-based fragrance companies can look back on an almost uninterrupted growth process from the post-war period to the end of the 20th century. From the time of the economic miracle until the 1990s, Dragoco and Haarmann & Reimer grew faster than the average for the German economy. There was a series of recession years; at the end of the economic miracle in 1967; later in 1973 and 1982 as a result of the oil crises; and in 1993 during the Gulf War. They did affect the Holzminden companies but they never led to a major slump. In most cases, the situation improved very quickly. Demand for products from Holzminden rose steadily until the end of the 1990s.

The prosperity of the companies was characterised by a unique security for the employees. Anyone who had found work at Haarmann & Reimer or Dragoco, and

Worldwide Growth

Dragoco's Management Board in 2000: Horst-Otto Gerberding, Roger F. Schmid, Daniel E. Stebbins and Dr. Richard Winter

as Works Council Chairman Harald Feist puts it in retrospect, "had not stolen any golden spoons", could be sure of their job. As a result, quite a few family dynasties developed among the workforce, with several generations of family members finding a job in the respective company. In the respective company, mind you, because changes between companies were contractually forbidden for qualified employees and frowned upon at least for ordinary workers.

At the end of the 20th century, the parameters changed, and in some cases dramatically. In the 2017 Corporate Atlas, the Heinrich Böll Foundation states: "*Since the 1980s, the transnational corporations that produce plant-based foods have continued to transform themselves into global players that are no longer only active in a few countries, but all over the world. [...] Today, a few global corporations determine the major trends in agriculture and food consumption.*" With the size and globalisation of these companies, the demands on suppliers have also grown. Ever larger quantities are required with consistent quality and rapid availability. Even for a company like Dragoco, which could boast of being the seventh or eighth largest company in the industry worldwide, it became difficult to fulfil these conditions. Haarmann & Reimer was somewhat better positioned in this respect due to its size and its connection to the Bayer Group, but it soon became clear that the connection to the Bayer Group would cause very serious problems in a completely different way.

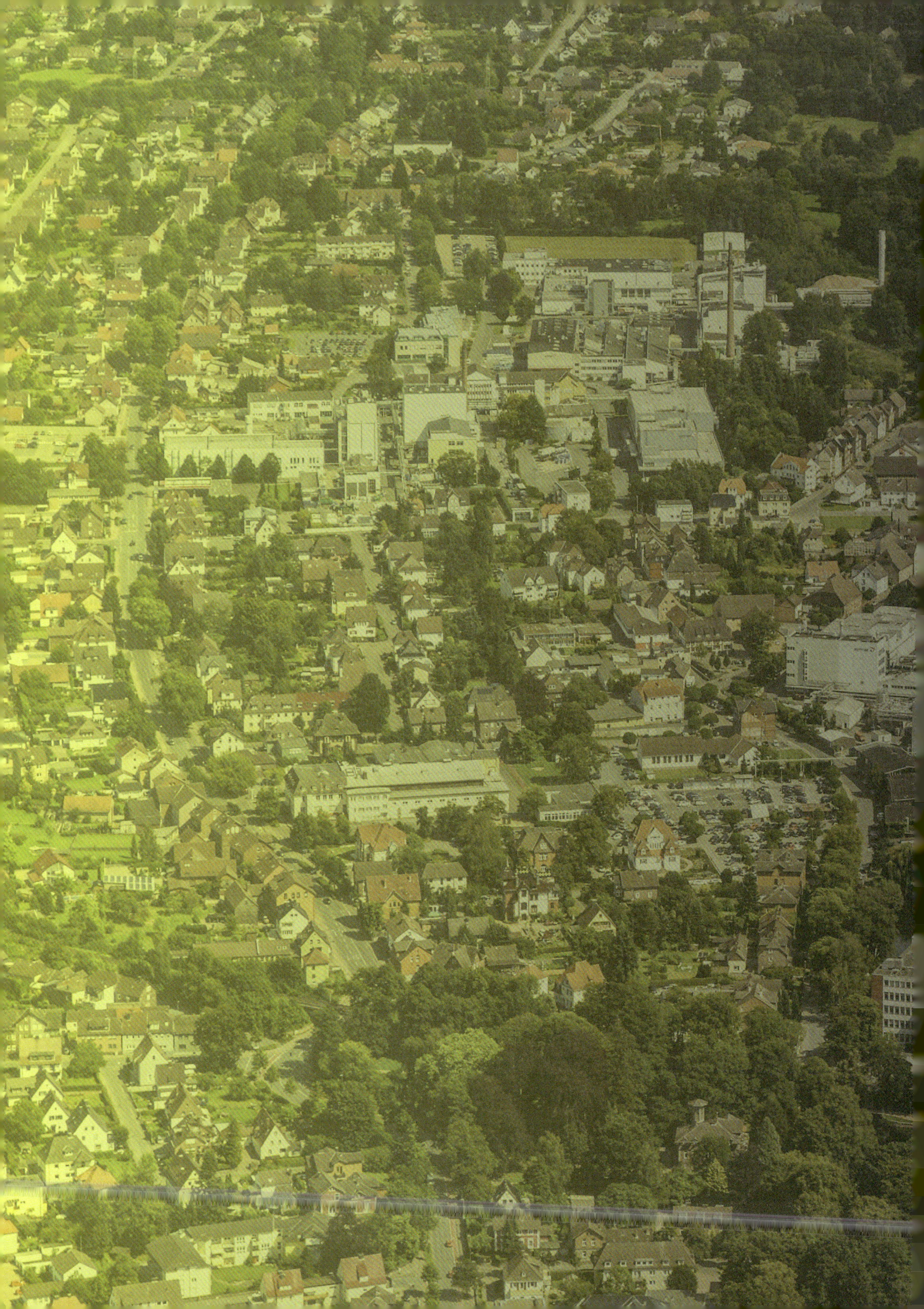

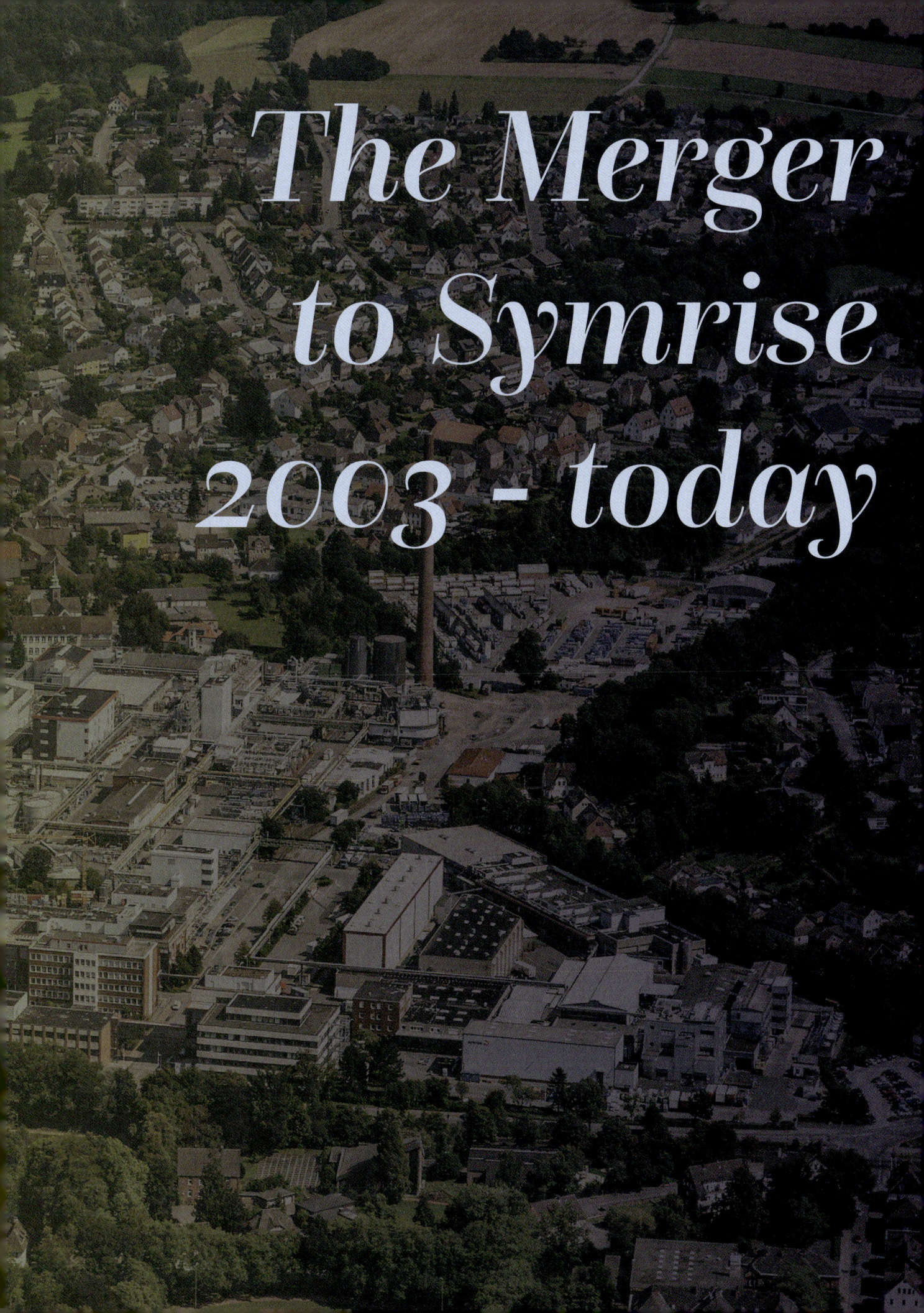

The Merger to Symrise
2003 - today

The merger of Haarmann & Reimer with Dragoco is reflected in the Symrise logo, where the dragon (Dragoco AG) and the hummingbird (H&R) – modelled on the ying-yang symbol – can be found.

The Merger to Symrise

In retrospect, historical narratives often read as being inevitable and continuous: 'It couldn't have happened any other way'. But perhaps it could have: the history of the fragrance and flavour industry in Holzminden could have ended 130 years later in 2004 or as early as 2002. With the announcement of the sale of its subsidiary Haarmann & Reimer at the end of 2001, Bayer, the parent company, shattered the alleged peace and tranquillity in the Weser town of Holzminden. It was not enough that three months earlier the whole world had been thrown into disarray by the attacks of 11 September 2001. In the following five years, there was great uncertainty in Holzminden regarding the future of the local fragrance and flavour industry. The years were dominated by the merger of a group-managed company with a family-run company under the control of a private financial investor. The intention of the investor EQT was to create synergies by merging the two companies in order to increase the value of the new company for a subsequent flotation on the public market: In order to increase profitability, the relocation of production to Eastern Europe was also considered. Many skilled employees left Holzminden during this time. In 2004, a major concession on the part of the employees led to an agreement to safeguard the site, which, however, meant a further reduction of the workforce by 350 employees. It was not until the stock market flotation in 2006 that Symrise entered somewhat calmer waters. After a period of austerity, the company expanded in the following years through acquisitions. Especially after Heinz Jürgen Bertram took over the position of CEO in 2009, the course of growth was intensified through further acquisitions. The company's portfolio was expanded and diversified in various directions.

With almost 3,000 employees at the Holzminden site, Symrise employed more people in 2024 than its predecessor companies Haarmann & Reimer and Dragoco ever did combined. Added to this are several hundred employees at the companies Th. Geyer Ingredients, NeoCos and ACS International, whose business activities are directly intertwined with Symrise. In retrospect, the merger that created Symrise must, therefore, be regarded as a success story. However, as things could have turned out very differently, it is very revealing to analyse which factors contributed to the success of this merger.

It all began in 2001 when Bayer wanted to sell Haarmann & Reimer
On 8 August 2001, Bayer withdrew Lipobay, a statin that had been a commercial success until then, from the market due to severe side effects with fatal consequences. After the problems became known, Bayer was sued in approximately 15,000 cases. In total, Bayer paid out more than one billion US dollars in settlements.

At the end of 2001, the decision was made to sell the profitable Group subsidiary Haarmann & Reimer in an open bidding process in order to compensate for the resulting economic imbalance.

On 16 August 2001, the Tagesschau reported on the criticism of Bayer because of the side effects of Lipobay.

Press release EU Commission
Brussels, 17 September 2002

Commission authorises EQT's acquisition of Haarmann & Reimer and Dragoco

In accordance with merger regulations, the European Commission has authorised the takeover of two German manufacturers of fragrances and flavourings, Haarmann & Reimer GmbH (H&R) and Dragoco Gerberding & Co. AG, by the private equity fund EQT, which is ultimately controlled by the Swedish investor group AB. According to the Commission's market analysis, competition in the European market for fragrances, flavours, aroma chemicals and cosmetic ingredients is sufficiently ensured even after the takeover. On 12 August 2002, the Commission received notification of the planned merger, which would give EQT Northern Europe control over all of Dragoco and Haarmann & Reimer through the purchase of shares and assets. The purchase is to be handled by Isis Vermögensverwaltung GmbH, a German-based asset management company set up specifically for this purpose. Haarmann & Reimer is currently owned by the German Bayer Group, while the majority shareholder of Dragoco is its CEO Horst-Otto Gerberding, who is selling his shares to Isis in return for a minority stake. Gerberding will take over the management of the new company.

EQT's corporate strategy is to invest in medium-sized companies and, thus, generate profits for its investors; EQT intends to float the company resulting from the merger of Haarmann & Reimer and Dragoco on the stock exchange. The two companies are based in Holzminden and produce fragrances and flavours, aroma chemicals and cosmetic ingredients; their future combined market share will not exceed 15%. The Commission has established that the customers of the products, in particular the food and beverage manufacturers and the cosmetics industry, will not become overly dependent on Haarmann & Reimer/Dragoco as they have access to suppliers throughout Europe and possibly even outside Europe. The Commission also took into account that there are important competitors on the market with the necessary know-how to produce a wide range of fragrances, flavours, aroma chemicals and cosmetic ingredients for a wide variety of end products.

The sale

Company acquisitions and takeovers run through the history of the Holzminden companies: Dragoco had already acquired the Heinrich Haensel company in 1935, thereby significantly expanding its own business. In the 1950s, Haarmann & Reimer and Dragoco took over the agencies of Schimmel & Co. And in 1954, Haarmann & Reimer was ultimately bought by Bayer. In the following decades, the sustained upswing associated with this purchase made further company acquisitions by Bayer possible, and these were integrated into the Haarmann & Reimer operations. Dragoco was also able to acquire a number of smaller companies in the industry in the post-war decades which could be integrated into the business. However, the sale of Haarmann & Reimer in 2002 took place under different circumstances. In view of the global concentration processes, Haarmann & Reimer found itself the focus of major competitors. There was, therefore, a real risk that the company would be taken over by a competitor and the Holzminden site would be converted into a pure production site.

How is the sale of a major company organised?

The future CEO Dr. Heinz Jürgen Bertram had just been promoted to head of research at Haarmann & Reimer when Bayer's decision to sell the company was announced. Together with the five other division heads, he had to present the company to potential buyers in the scheduled bidding process. While in normal trade it is precisely a matter of publicising the technical specifications and capabilities of an object and, thus, convincing the buyer, a delicate situation arises when selling a company, where the main focus is on keeping recipes and processes secret. This is because the secrets must inevitably also be revealed to those who do not ultimately buy the company. Heinz Jürgen Bertram remembers that individual interested parties came to the sales talks in 'army strength'. Some of the companies also came with a large number of employees to the 'data room', where interested parties were able to take a look at the files containing the most important business data. Neither Deutsche Bank, under whose leadership the proceedings were conducted, nor Haarmann & Reimer itself could have guaranteed that all sensitive information could be protected from being copied in view of the large number of files. According to Dr Bertram, the process in the first half of 2002 was leading to the world market leader from Switzerland, Givaudan, buying Haarmann & Reimer. Trade media also reported that Givaudan was very interested in the Holzminden-based company. Private equity companies had also shown interest, but had already dropped out at an earlier stage of the process. Since Givaudan bought Quest, a similarly large competitor, a few years later, it can be assumed that the purchase of Haarmann & Reimer would also have been authorised under the cartel law.

The world's largest companies in fragrance and flavour production: Mergers and mergers have significantly changed the structure of the industry in recent years:

International Flavors & Fragrances Inc., USA, founded in 1958, announced in 2021 that it was merging with the Nutrition & Biosciences division of the US chemicals group DuPont. The merger created the world's largest supplier of fragrances and flavours, and **Firmenich International SA**, Switzerland, founded in 1895, merged with the Dutch chemical company DSM in 2023. DSM-Firmenich is now the No. 2 in the industry in terms of sales. **Givaudan SA**, Switzerland, founded in 1895, the long-standing industry leader now ranks third.

Symrise AG now ranks fourth in the fragrances and flavours market in terms of sales.

EQT

EQT Partners AB is a venture capital and private equity investment group operating primarily in Northern Europe and Asia. Its headquarters are in Stockholm and it was founded in 1994 by the Swedish investor AB. The company has been listed on the Stockholm Stock Exchange since September 2019.
EQT primarily acquires or finances well-positioned, medium-sized companies through its funds and seeks to sustainably develop their market position, thus increasing the value of the company. The ultimate goal is to sell the company or take it public.
To date, EQT has raised a total of EUR 38 billion in equity capital from over 400 investors and has invested EUR 22 billion of this in 170 companies. The company now has offices in 16 countries with approximately 700 employees.

2001 – Private equity companies were showing interest in Dragoco

Although Dragoco's figures were quite good, the owner family Gerberding was concerned about the further successful development of the company. Dragoco ranked seventh among fragrance and flavour manufacturers worldwide. Similar to other industries, the large global corporations had reduced their number of suppliers from three to five. In view of the concentration processes, it was clear to everyone involved that Dragoco would come under increasing pressure.

2002 – The merger idea was born

By his own admission, Horst-Otto Gerberding rejected the initial advances made by EQT and another private equity company in 2001, so EQT initially participated in the bidding process with another company in the industry. At that time, EQT's idea was to split the company into a perfumery house with cosmetics and chemical production segments, as well as a flavour house. However, when the partner withdrew, EQT approached Horst Otto Gerberding and Dragoco again. After Easter 2002, EQT finally reached an agreement with the owners of Dragoco to enter the bidding process and to merge the two companies once EQT had acquired Haarmann & Reimer.

EQT would acquire a minority stake in Dragoco and Horst-Otto Gerberding would then contribute his shares to the newly created company. He agreed to this after some consideration and instigated a corresponding supervisory board decision. As EQT was acting as the buyer, Gerberding was not allowed to participate in the negotiations with Bayer and was also not given any insight into the internal figures of Haarmann & Reimer. To ensure that the process would be positive for the company and for the Holzminden location, Horst-Otto Gerberding contacted Minister President Gabriel of the State Government of Lower Saxony, the chairman of the BCE industrial union (founded in 1997 as the Mining, Chemical and Energy Industrial Union), and Bayer supervisory board member Mr. Schmoldt. Karl-Heinz Huchthausen, chairman of the Haarmann & Reimer works council, was also informed of the merger plans via the Bayer works council and judged them to be essentially positive. As a member of the general works council of Bayer AG, Huchthausen was well connected and exchanged views on this topic with the Chairman of the BCE industrial union Hubertus Schmoldt, who sat on the supervisory board of Bayer AG as an employee representative. As Huchthausen saw the merger as the best possible solution for the company, the employee representatives at Bayer were in favour of this solution.

The Merger to Symrise

Bid accepted in favour of EQT for EUR 1.66 billion

EQT was ultimately awarded the right to purchase Haarmann & Reimer as part of the open bidding process. At the same time, EQT acquired a minority stake in Dragoco. The involvement of politicians and industrial unions may have tipped the scales, as EQT had clearly not offered the highest price and also received a loan from Bayer.

On 17 July 2002, EQT published a press release stating that Haarmann & Reimer and Dragoco would be merged by EQT to form a new company. EQT held 76%, Horst-Otto Gerberding 22% and Nord/LB 2% of the new company. The purchase price for Haarmann & Reimer was €1.66 billion. Horst-Otto Gerberding became managing director and Haarmann & Reimer Managing Director Lambert Courth returned to Bayer.

2003 – Official merger in February

On 20 February 2003, the two Holzminden-based companies Dragoco AG (now the Solling plant) and Haarmann & Reimer (H&R, now the Weser plant) merged. This merger resulted in the new company named Symrise GmbH & Co. KG. The merger of the two companies is also reflected in the Symrise logo which is based on the yin and yang symbol and in which the dragon (Dragoco AG) and the hummingbird (Haarmann & Reimer) can be found. The newly created name Symrise is a combination of the words symbiosis and arise. With sales of 1.245 billion euros and 5,800 employees, Symrise became the world's fourth-largest company in the fragrance and flavour industry in 2002.

Merger of a group-managed company with a family business

The merger of the two companies, which operated at the same location but were in competition, was a challenging task. Different corporate cultures had to be brought together and prejudices that had been cultivated for decades had to be overcome. In April 2003, a first *"global management meeting"* was held to develop a *"corporate code of conduct that is to be binding for all employees of the Symrise Group"*. Horst-Otto Gerberding then addressed the employees of Symrise in a letter. Among other things, it stated:

It was only after the merger that everyone involved realised how well the two companies fitted together: The strengths and weaknesses in the flavour and fragrance segments complemented each other almost perfectly.

2003 – 2024

"*EQT has no interest in extracting short-term profits from the company which would have consequences for the company's cash flow and investment behaviour. It is rather the aim to float the company on the stock exchange in 3-5 years - provided that continuous growth in sales and earnings can be achieved. In this context, I would like to emphasise once again how important it is to achieve the budget!*" On 15 September 2003, Horst-Otto Gerberding moved to the advisory board of Symrise. He was succeeded as managing director by James D. Forman from September 2003 to February 2005.

„What belongs together has not yet grown together"

The situation in Holzminden was highlighted in a report in the Hannoversche Allgemeine Zeitung, the Hannover based newspaper, on 6 March 2004 under the headline '*Neither leadership nor a clear line visible*'. Lars Ruzic, the author, wrote: "*It is currently the most exciting merger process in Lower Saxony. Even almost a year after the Symrise Group was formed from the Holzminden-based neighbours Haarmann & Reimer and Dragoco, the two companies have not yet grown together. There is great uncertainty amongst the workforce. [...] For more than 80 years, generations of Holzminden residents worked either at the family-run Dragoco company or at the Bayer subsidiary H&R. Switching jobs between companies was frowned upon. Each company suffered from the paranoia that the other might find out something more about them. After all, their industry is one of the most secretive of all. The major manufacturers of fragrances, flavours and cosmetic ingredients can be counted on one hand. Their customers demand confidentiality - often not even the employee knows exactly for which perfume brand he is putting together the essence. The automotive supplier sector, by contrast, is quite gossipy.*"

In view of this analysis, it is no wonder that the merger was difficult to achieve. The transfer of Horst Otto Gerberding to the advisory board in 2003 contributed to further uncertainty among the workforce. However, the new managing director, US-American James D. Forman, who joined Symrise from Stollwerck, was viewed critically by the author of the press article. The article claimed that "*neither a clear line nor leadership can be recognised.*" It continued: "*In the first few months, the employees didn't even get to see Forman. He was like a phantom*". The article throws a spotlight on the mood at Symrise in Holzminden at the time, as it concluded with a statement on the decision to cut jobs: "*'And since the markets will not change significantly,' says a Symrise insider, 'profit growth will have to come mainly from cost-cutting measures.' Symrise employees are, therefore, sceptical as to whether the last word has already been spoken on job cuts. At least on this issue, there is no difference between the 'Weser plant' and the 'Solling plant',*" wrote Lars Ruzic in the Hannover newpaper.

Work on a spray dryer at Symrise in Holzminden

MITTWOCH, 17. NOVEMBER 2004   **STADT UND LANDKREIS — HOLZMINDEN**   SEITE 17

Symrise investiert 46 Mio. Euro in den Standort Holzminden!

325 Stellen werden abgebaut / Wiedereinführung der 40-Stunden-Woche / Trotzdem Beifall von der Belegschaft

Holzminden (rei). Die Geschäftsführung nennt es „Prozessoptimierung" oder „Maßnahmen zur Steigerung der Wettbewerbsfähigkeit", Betriebsrat und Landesregierung reden von „Sicherung des Standortes und der Arbeitsplätze". Aber so unterschiedlich Sichtweise und Motivation auch sein mögen: Die meisten Symrise-Mitarbeiter kamen gestern kurz nach 15 Uhr mit zufriedenem Gesicht aus der Stadthalle. Und das, obwohl man ihnen gerade mitgeteilt hatte, dass sie demnächst wieder 40 Stunden die Woche arbeiten müssen, dass es zwei Jahre lang keine Lohnerhöhungen gibt und dass weitere 325 Stellen abgebaut werden sollen. Was diese negativen Nachrichten in den Schatten stellte, war eine Zahl: Symrise wird in den nächsten drei Jahren in Holzminden für rund 46 Millionen Euro investieren!

„Es knisterte förmlich vor Spannung im Saal", beschrieb Niedersachsens Innenminister Uwe Schünemann in dem anschließenden Pressegespräch die Stimmung zu Beginn der Informationsveranstaltung. Nach Bekanntgabe der Entscheidungen der Geschäftsführung sei Erleichterung zu spüren gewesen. Es war der wichtigste Tag für das Unternehmen seit der Fusion vor gut zwei Jahren. Die Mitarbeiter wussten: Es steht sehr viel auf dem Spiel. Seit Geschäftsführer James D. Forman im Juni verkündet hatte, dass auch an Produktionsverlagerungen in Billiglohnländer gedacht werde, ging die Angst um in Holzminden - nicht nur innerhalb der Belegschaft.

Was seitdem hinter den Kulissen gelaufen ist, lässt sich nur erahnen. Fest steht, dass fast bis zum letzten Tag vor der Infoveranstaltung noch verhandelt wurde. Die „Verhandlungsbasis" wäre für Holzminden eine Katastrophe geworden: Verlagerung von weiten Teilen der Produktion nach Polen oder in die Slowakei, verbunden damit ein Abbau von fast 950 Stellen. Dieses „Horrorszenario" konnte durch die Gemeinschaftsleistung abgewendet werden, die Ministerpräsident Christian Wulff als „Modellfall für Deutschland" bezeichnete. Er kam gestern persönlich nach Holzminden, um seine Zufriedenheit über das Verhandlungsergebnis kund zu tun - und brachte gleich noch drei seiner Minister mit. Neben Uwe Schünemann saßen Wirtschaftsminister Walter Hirche und Umweltminister Hans-Heinrich Sander in der ersten Reihe.

Geschäftsführung, Betriebsrat und Gewerkschaft haben in den letzten Monaten ein Paket geschnürt, das die Investoren offenbar überzeugt hat. Rückkehr zur 40-Stunden-Woche ohne Lohnausgleich und Verzicht auf Lohnerhöhungen in den nächsten zwei Jahren sind wohl die einschneidendsten Beiträge, die die Mitarbeiter für dieses Paket leisten. Die 325 Stellen, die bis Ende 2006 noch abgebaut werden sollen, sind natürlich auch ein schwerer Brocken. Doch der Betriebsrat hofft, hierfür sozialverträgliche Lösungen zu finden. Übrigens: „Die verabschiedeten Maßnahmen gelten für alle Mitarbeiter des Unternehmens, auch für Management und Geschäftsführung", heißt es ausdrücklich in der von Symrise versandten Pressemitteilung.

Beeindruckt hat die Investoren bei ihrer Entscheidungsfindung aber offenbar auch der Einsatz der Landesregierung. Nicht nur, dass sie die Verhandlungen aktiv begleitet hat, sie wird sich auch finanziell engagieren - mit erheblichen Zuschüssen zu den geplanten Investitionen.

Holzminden. Gespannte Gesichter vor der Infoveranstaltung in der Stadthalle. Übrigens wurden die Mitarbeiter auf der Einladung auch gebeten, „von Kommentaren und Aussagen gegenüber der Presse Abstand zu nehmen"... Foto: rei

„Das macht man nicht nur für fünf Jahre"

Geschäftsführung, Betriebsrat und Minister äußern sich zufrieden gegenüber der Presse

Holzminden (rei). „Ich bin äußerst glücklich für das Unternehmen und seine Mitarbeiter", betonte Symrise-Geschäftsführer James D. Forman direkt im Anschluss an die Informationsveranstaltung gegenüber der Presse. Nicht nur das große Medienecho, auch die Anwesenheit der Minister Hirche und Schünemann in der Pressekonferenz unterstrich die Bedeutung dieses Termins für die Stadt Holzminden, für die Region und für das ganze Land Niedersachsen.

Von zahlreichen Gesprächen in den letzten vier Monaten berichtete Betriebsratsvorsitzender Karl-Heinz Huchthausen. Das Ergebnis sei bei der Belegschaft positiv angekommen, es habe sogar Beifall in der Stadthalle gegeben. Er selbst bezeichnete das Ergebnis als „vertretbaren Kompromiss", der die Arbeitsplätze in Holzminden und Nordlingen sichere. Der geplante Stellenabbau lasse sich nach seiner Einschätzung sozial verträglich gestalten. Huchthausen rechnete vor: 200 befristete Verträge laufen aus, 100 Mitarbeiter könnten in Altersteilzeit gehen, anderen würde man Teilzeitangebote machen können.

Wirtschaftsminister Hirche wertete die Entscheidungen als Signal, dass die Wettbewerbsfähigkeit in Deutschland eine Zukunft habe. 46 Millionen Euro zu investieren, sei mehr als die Absicherung von Arbeitsplätzen - „hier wird nach vorn gegangen". „Das macht man nicht nur für fünf Jahre", so des Ministers Hoffnung. Ein großes Lob gebühre Betriebsrat und Belegschaft, „ihre Art von Flexibilität und Hartnäckigkeit bringt den Standort nach vorn".

Innenminister Schünemann, selbst einst H&R-Mitarbeiter, war die Erleichterung deutlich anzumerken. Vor einem halben Jahr hätte er sich diese Art von Flexibilität und Zusammenarbeit nicht vorstellen können. Was hier erreicht wurde - ohne Arbeitskampf oder ähnliche Aktivitäten - zeige auch, wie sehr die Region mit der Firma verhaftet sei. Das alles werde positiv auf die Belegschaft wirken und das Betriebsklima sicher wieder deutlich verbessern. „Für die Region wäre ein unaufholbarer Schaden entstanden, wenn 950 Arbeitsplätze weggefallen wären", so der Holzmindener Minister.

Die 46 Millionen Euro würden letztlich noch viel mehr in der Region auslösen, man denke nur an die Aufträge fürs Handwerk. Ministerpräsident Wulff habe übrigens seine Hilfe angeboten, wenn es den betriebsbedingten Kündigungen kommt.

James D. Forman wirkte ebenfalls erleichtert. Er gab zu bedenken: „Wir sind in den Händen von Privatinvestoren, und es ist keine leichte Aufgabe, Investoren zu überzeugen." Er bestätigte, dass man sich „in allen osteuropäischen Ländern" nach möglichen Produktionsstandorten umgesehen habe. Polen und die Slowakei kamen in die engere Wahl, das Lohnkosten-Verhältnis zu Deutschland beträgt hier etwa 1:8. Letztlich müsse bei einem solchen „Umzug" aber auch berücksichtigt werden, nämlich auch die Qualitätssicherung, das Image und die Resonanz bei den Kunden. „Wir denken alle international. Aber das Know how ist man hat seit drei bis vier Generationen hier in Holzminden!", so der Geschäftsführer. Minister Schünemann ergänzte: „Hier weiß man, was man hat!"

Die 46 Millionen sollen übrigens innerhalb der nächsten drei Jahre investiert werden, und zwar hauptsächlich in drei große Projekte: Zusammenlegung beziehungsweise Neubau der Bereiche Fragances und „natürliche Aromen" sowie des Pulvermischbetriebes (noch gibt es jeweils in den Werken „Weser" und „Solling") mit Logistiklager.

Wie hoch die Zuschüsse des Landes werden, wollte Minister Hirche nicht sagen. Das richte sich nach den jeweiligen Förderanträgen, es geht vor allem um Mittel aus den Töpfen „Gemeinschaftsaufgabe regionale Wirtschaftsförderung" und „Ziel-2". Er bestätigte, dass das Unternehmen im Falle der Förderung gewisse Auflagen erfüllen müsse - zum Beispiel Arbeitsplatzsicherung für fünf Jahre. „Kann ein liberaler Minister damit leben, ein gesundes Unternehmen zu bezuschussen?", wollte die Presse wissen. Hirche verteidigte die Haltung der Landesregierung: Besser jetzt helfen, als später, wenn es vielleicht zu spät ist.

Zuletzt sprach der TAH das Thema „Börsengang" an. Doch eine Antwort gab es nicht. „Ich bin nicht in der Lage, heute was dazu zu sagen", so James D. Forman.

ANZEIGE

Suche Geländewagen
Pick up und Pkw, auch defekt
oder Unfall
Tel. (0 55 51) 91 11 99 (Hdl.)

„Ein Modellfall für Deutschland"

Christian Wulff lobt Flexibilität der Belegschaft

Holzminden (rei). Trotz übervollen Terminkalenders ließ es sich Ministerpräsident Christian Wulff nicht nehmen, gestern in der Stadthalle persönlich zu den Mitarbeitern von Symrise zu sprechen und damit die Bedeutung dieser Unternehmensentscheidung für die Menschen in der ganzen Region zu unterstreichen. Gegenüber dem TAH nahm er am Rande der Veranstaltung kurz Stellung.

„Eine große Phase der Verunsicherung geht zu Ende", kommentierte Wulff den Prozess seit der Fusion von H&R und Dragoco bis zum heutigen Tag. Dass es statt einer Verlagerung nach Mittel- und Osteuropa nun zu einer Entscheidung für den Standort Holzminden gekommen sei, war laut Wulff nur möglich, „weil alle an einem Strang gezogen haben". Dafür sei allen Beteiligten zu danken - besonders der Belegschaft für eine hohe Flexibilität, aber auch den Eigentümern für ihre „Sensibilität für den Standort". Besonders hob der Ministerpräsident außerdem den Betriebsratsvorsitzenden Karl-Heinz Huchthausen und mit ihm die IG BCE hervor.

Nach dem Abschluss des VW-Tarifes gehe von Symrise ein weiteres tolles Signal aus für die Wettbewerbsfähigkeit des Standortes Deutschland. Wulff nannte Symrise sogar einen „Modellfall für Deutschland".

Natürlich sprach er auch das Engagement der Landesregierung an. Sie wisse, wie wichtig dieser Arbeitgeber für die ganze Region sei und wie sehr sich die Region mit Symrise identifiziere. Darum habe die Landesregierung alle ihre Möglichkeiten ausgeschöpft, um sich für den Erhalt des Standortes und damit der Arbeitsplätze einzusetzen.

Dieses enge Zusammenwirken von Land, Betriebsrat, Gewerkschaft, Geschäftsführung und Beirat habe letztlich zum Erfolg geführt.

Christian Wulff.

Zentnerlast vom Herzen gefallen

Holzminden (rei). „Mir fällt eine Zentnerlast vom Herzen, ich bin heilfroh und freue mich für die Menschen in der Region" - überschwänglich kommentierte Holzmindens Bürgermeister Dr. Wolfgang Bönig gestern Nachmittag die Entscheidungen bei Symrise. Sein besonderer Dank für ihren „unglaublichen Einsatz" galt dem Betriebsratsvorsitzenden Karl-Heinz Huchthausen und Niedersachsens Innenminister Uwe Schünemann.

Dr. Wolfgang Bönig.

Holzminden. Betriebsrat, Geschäftsführung und Landesregierung standen der Presse Rede und Antwort. Foto: rei

Report in the Täglicher Anzeiger Holzminden about the works meeting on 16 November 2004

2004 – No relocation of production
Negotiations with the works council save the Holzminden site

The worries and uncertainty among the employees and residents of the region were, therefore, considerable. It was in light of these circumstances that the relocation of production to Eastern Europe proposed by EQT was negotiated in autumn 2004. The Lower Saxony State Government was also involved in these negotiations between the works council, management and executive board. On 17 November 2004, Tägliche Anzeiger Holzminden (TAH), the local newspaper, reported on the works meeting held the day before, at which the result of the negotiations was announced, and on the subsequent press conference. The event was also attended by Lower Saxony's Minister President Christian Wulff, Interior Minister Uwe Schünemann and Environment Minister Hans-Heinrich Sander, who both come from the area, and Economics Minister Walter Hirche. As a result of the negotiations, management was able to announce that a previous plan to relocate production to Eastern Europe had been dropped. The TAH wrote about this: "*Management calls it 'process optimisation' or 'measures to increase competitiveness'. The works council and state government talk about 'securing the location and jobs'. But as different as the perspective and motivation may be: Most Symrise employees came out of the town hall shortly after 3 p.m. yesterday with a satisfied look on their faces. And this was despite the fact that they had just been told they would soon have to work 40 hours a week again; there would be no pay rise for two years; and a further 325 jobs were to be cut. What overshadowed this negative news was one figure: Symrise will invest around 46 million euros in Holzminden over the next three years!*" The "*horror scenario*" of the relocation of production had been averted by a joint effort, which Lower Saxony's Minister President Wulff described as a "*model case for Germany*" at the subsequent press conference. This was possible "*because everyone had worked as one*". Wulff thanked everyone involved, especially the staff for their high degree of flexibility, but also the owners for their "*sensitivity to the location*". "*The Minister President also made special mention of Works Council Chairman Karl-Heinz Huchthausen and the BCE industrial union,*" the TAH report continued. Symrise Managing Director James D. Forman was quoted as saying: "*I am extremely happy for the company and its employees.*" Karl-Heinz Huchthausen was cited on the further planned job cuts, explaining that 200 fixed-term contracts would expire, 100 employees could go into partial retirement and others would also be offered part-time work so that this could be organised in a socially responsible manner. The willingness of the state to subsidise Symrise's investments with additional millions was a positive factor in the outcome of the negotiations. In 2024, Karl-Heinz Huchthausen said that this money had never been called upon.

Company headquarter in Holzminden

Tesium and Symotion

In order to further improve Symrise's competitiveness in the run-up to its flotation on the public market, the owners and management proposed outsourcing parts of the company. The focus was on technology, logistics and IT. While IT was, in fact, outsourced to the IT service provider Atos Origin, the establishment of the subsidiaries Tesium and Symotion meant that the other two areas could remain in Holzminden. This solution was agreed by the works council, the BCE industrial union, and the management and in October 2004 became part of the location security contract with an initial term of five years. After that, the contract was extended twice more, each time for five years. It is to be replaced by new collective agreements from 2025.

2006 – Symrise was floated on the public market

In 2005, Symrise with CEO Gerold Linzbach, who replaced James D. Forman in March, and around 4800 employees achieved sales of 1.15 billion euros. Since the merger, the number of employees had been reduced by around 1000. The company had been streamlined and made 'fit to sell'. In addition to the measures described above two production facilities in Skokie (Illinois) and Grasse were closed, as well as the creative perfumery centre in the heart of Hamburg. The company's various divisions were restructured. The two divisions Scent & Care and Flavours (now Taste, Nutrition & Health) were created, each of roughly the same size. The company went public in December 2006. The shares were included in the MDAX in March 2007. From the point of view of Dr. Heinz Jürgen Bertram, the Symrise company was "saved onto the stock exchange". The key company figures were only achieved through cost-cutting measures.

Symrise Jahres-Schlusskurse

Jahr	Erster	Hoch	Tief	Schluss	Veränderung
2024	99,48	120,60	92,34	120,10	20,73%
2023	101,80	109,80	87,90	99,48	-2,28%
2022	130,95	131,60	94,30	101,80	-22,26%
2021	109,40	132,00	96,64	130,95	19,70%
2020	93,90	120,50	73,90	109,40	16,51%
2019	65,06	93,90	64,48	93,90	44,33%
2018	71,39	81,50	62,40	65,06	-8,86%
2017	57,92	72,40	54,50	71,39	23,26%
2016	61,44	68,49	54,13	57,92	-5,74%
2015	50,08	64,02	49,56	61,44	22,69%
2014	33,53	50,61	33,51	50,08	49,36%
2013	27,07	35,07	26,05	33,53	23,87%
2012	20,55	27,83	20,55	27,07	31,72%
2011	20,48	22,75	16,37	20,55	0,37%
2010	15,00	22,36	15,00	20,48	36,50%
2009	9,93	15,75	7,10	15,00	51,06%
2008	19,00	18,90	7,86	9,93	-47,74%
2007	19,56	22,23	17,52	19,00	-2,86%
2006	18,48	19,84	18,48	19,56	5,84%

Table of Symrise annual closing prices on the Frankfurt Stock Exchange (2024: as of September, source: www.boerse.de)

Share and shareholder structure (current)
Massachusetts Financial Services Company (MFS) 9,96 %
BlackRock Inc. 6,07 %
Ministry of Finance on behalf of the State of Norway 5,05 %
Horst-Otto Gerberding 5,024 %
Canada Pension Plan Investment Board 4,97 %
APG Asset Management N.V. 3,01 %

Companies in the Symrise environment

In the course of history, similar companies have repeatedly been established in the vicinity of the two major manufacturers of fragrances and flavourings, Dragoco and Haarmann & Reimer. They then either focused on specialising further or catered to customer requests that could not be fulfilled by the two large companies. After the merger to form Symrise, numerous employees resigned or were laid off due to the austerity measures, or a number of processes were outsourced. However, due to the strong growth of Symrise since the 2010s, the regional companies in the global player's environment have also grown and more were newly established. In addition to Symrise, several hundred people are now employed in the fragrance and flavour industry in the region.

Th. Geyer Ingredients

Theodor Geyer, born in 1838, worked for the company C.F. Boehringer & Söhne, from which Böhringer Ingelheim and Boehringer Mannheim later emerged. The growth in the chemical industry prompted Theodor Geyer to found a chemicals business in Stuttgart on 15 October 1892. The small company grew and was able to survive in the market even in the following decades, which were marked by crises. In the 1950s, the company specialised in laboratory chemicals, which is still the core business at the site in Swabia today. However, in 1972, another segment was added when a cooperation agreement was signed with Haarmann & Reimer to distribute flavours and fragrances. Incidentally, a postcard in Geyer's company archives proves that a business contact existed 77 years before the start of that collaboration when the company ordered "1-2 kg vanillin" from Haarmann & Reimer.

Until the merger that created Symrise, Geyer was able to handle the distribution of Haarmann & Reimer products from Stuttgart and Renningen. After the merger, business with Symrise developed in leaps and bounds. As a distribution partner of Symrise, Th. Geyer also supplies smaller customers with the product portfolio of the large company. In 2009, the company moved into a new building in Stahle, in close proximity to Symrise. In 2010, Th. Geyer Ingredients GmbH & Co. KG was founded as a subsidiary "with the corporate purpose of development, sales and distribution of additives, substances and ingredients for products in the pharmaceutical, cosmetics and food industries, as well as other industries". In 2014, the product portfolio was subdivided into the areas of Food & Beverages and

Scent & Care. Between 2014 and 2019, the Höxter-Stahle site was significantly expanded and new brands were introduced for specialised product lines. Th. Geyer in Stahle now employs almost 150 people.

However, Geyer did not only maintain contacts with the fragrance and flavour industry. The FLORAL brand, under which Th. Geyer now manufactures leather care products at the Stahle site, originates from a completely different regional connection. Originally, FLORAL was a brand of the Florida chemistry company, which was founded in Holzminden in 1960 and later taken over by the Gregor chemistry company. Originally, cosmetics and household products were also sold under the FLORAL brand in addition to leather care. Today, only shoe polish is still produced. In 2016, after Th. Geyer took over the Gregor chemical company and with it their trademark rights, the traditional production of shoe care products in Stahle could be continued.

NeoCos Service GmbH

NeoCos Service specialises in the development and manufacture of quality-assured cosmetic products in different batch sizes. Wilhelm Kühn, a chemist and cosmetics developer formerly employed by Haarmann & Reimer, recognised that cosmetics brands initially wanted to purchase smaller quantities of newly developed products. Together with his wife Petra Kühn, he founded Neo Cos Service GmbH in 1991 as a service provider in the field of professional and exclusive active cosmetics.

In 2017, the company moved into its specially designed new building at the Stahle site with over 7,000 m² of production and storage space. Around 60 people are employed there.

ACSInternational

The founding of Aroma Chemical Services International GmbH in 2004 can be directly traced back to the merger of Haarmann & Reimer and Dragoco to form Symrise. Two former Haarmann & Reimer employees started out as a commercial agency, using their extensive industry network and existing contacts as their initial capital. In 2006, a production company in Romania was acquired. ACS employs around 95 people at the Romanian site in Onesti.

Biotechnological manufacturing processes and peroxide chemistry processes are used there for the production of various macrocyclic musk fragrances and other speciality fragrances.

The site in Stahle, in the immediate vicinity of Geyer and NeoCos, forms the distribution centre. Around 30 people are employed there.

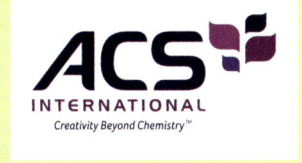

Other Companies ...

Heinz Jürgen Bertram - CEO from 2009 to 2024

In summer 2009, Heinz Jürgen Bertram replaced Gerold Linzbach as CEO. Linzbach did not want to extend the contract *"for personal reasons"*. Like Forman, Linzbach did not really warm to the company headquarters in Holzminden. In this respect, the choice of Heinz Jürgen Bertram was much better suited to the location: With a PhD in chemistry and his roots in Holzminden, he had a much deeper connection to the company and its employees, which is one of the reasons why the works council of that time supported his election. Despite its supposedly down-to-earth nature, the company developed around its core business in some unexpected directions in the 15 years under the management of Heinz Jürgen Bertram. In 2015, after the successful billion-euro acquisition of the French pet food specialist *Diana*, for which he was responsible, Bertram said in an interview: *"In 2008, 10% of our business was outside of flavour and fragrances, today it is already more than 30% - and by 2028, we want to generate more than half of our sales outside of the traditional business to achieve our new goals. This diversification was and is crucial to our success."* Bertram cited the company's innovative strength as another success factor. The establishment of the perfumery school in Holzminden should also be seen in this context. The company now also has its own perfumery school in India. With these perfumery schools, the company is building on similar training centres that Dragoco established in Holzminden in the 1980s. In addition to the research centre in Holzminden, the company operates further development and research centres in France, Brazil, China, Singapore and the USA. Heinz Jürgen Bertram has been honoured as 'CEO of the Year' several times in his career. Under his leadership, the Symrise Group has grown enormously and has been able to consolidate its market position in various areas. However, Bertram was repeatedly criticised by employees for the fact that the company's profits benefit the shareholders more than the employees.

Heinz-Jürgen Bertram, photo from *moments / 10 years symrise*

"Onto the DAX and away from the collective agreement contract?"

Under this motto, the BCE industrial union, together with the general works council of Symrise, Tesium and Symotion, called for a demonstration in the Holzminden pedestrian zone on Saturday, 21 August 2021. The reason for this was the cancellation of collective bargaining negotiations by the company management. In view of the company's rising profits and the targeted promotion of the Symrise share to the DAX, the BCE industrial union had revoked the location protection agreement negotiated in 2009 in order to give the employees a share in the company's success. The aim was to roduco the working week from 40 hours and bring wages in line with the collective industrial agreement. 500 demonstrators showed that the union could count on

On Monday, 23 August 2021, the Täglicher Anzeiger Holzminden reported on the protest rally by Symrise employees organised by IG BCE.

broad support from the employees. The goal of resuming negotiations was also achieved, and a new company collective agreement was agreed with a large number of improvements for the employees; the company management only remained firm on the weekly working hours as the 40-hour week still applies at Symrise. In view of an EBIT margin of just under or over 20% and dividend increases for shareholders, it is still incomprehensible for many Symrise employees that they do not receive a greater share of the profits.

Heinz Jürgen Bertram counters this argument by saying that the reality on the stock market must be recognised. If the company loses market value, there is a risk of a takeover by a competitor.

2021 – Symrise moved up to the DAX and continued to grow

Symrise AG was included in the German benchmark index DAX on 20 September 2021. The company continued to grow through further acquisitions in the food and animal feed sectors and sales of € 3.8 billion were achieved in 2021. At the same time, the operating business was restructured and organised into two segments: Taste, Nutrition & Health and Scent & Care. Compared to the past, when only flavourings were produced, Symrise now also supplied food supplements and animal feed in addition to flavourings. In the fragrance sector, the portfolio had been expanded to include not only perfumes, but also ingredients for personal care products.

In March 2022, Symrise also strengthened its fine fragrance business with two further acquisitions. Symrise also acquired stakes in two major biotechnology companies. At the end of the year, Symrise achieved sales of € 4.6 billion with more than 12,000 employees.

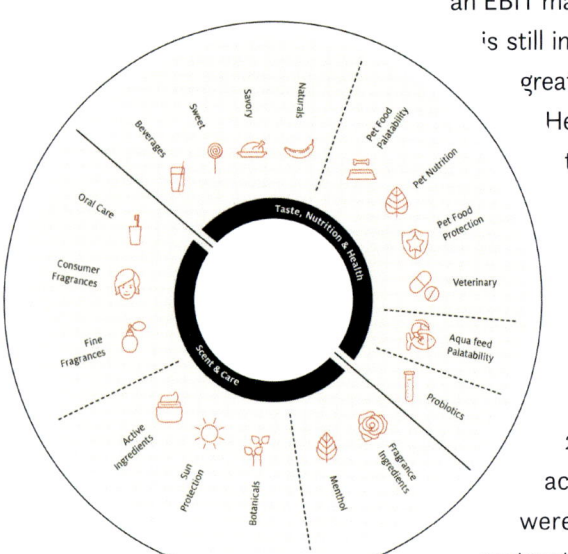

Presentation of the Symrise divisions
2006 (above),
2023 (below)

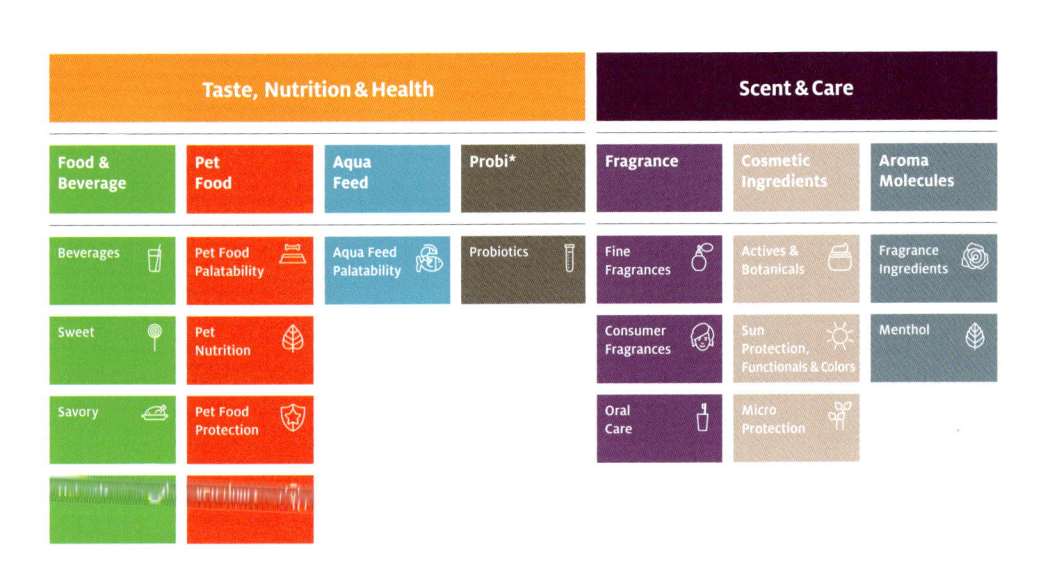

The Merger to Symrise

Research and patent protection

With around 2,000 employees, Symrise's research and development department is very well developed compared to other sectors. This has always been the real capital of the industry and is also demonstrated by the large number of patents that Symrise registers every year. Symrise's annual filing volume is usually around 30 to 70 initial applications per year. In 2024, Symrise had a total of 4,817 patents and patent applications worldwide, including all patents and patent applications in all countries for one invention. A total of 825 Symrise inventions are protected by patent law. In contrast to the past, patents no longer have to be registered for individual countries. Dr. Sven Siegel, director of global intellectual property, writes: "Whereas we used to have protection in very few countries, we now apply for patents in many regions, particularly in Europe, North and South America and Asia. Within Europe, filing strategies via the European Patent Office have become very important, and we use them almost 100% of the time." Siegel estimates the number of people monitoring possible patent infringements at "several hundred, if not thousands" while employees in many departments are constantly keeping their eyes and ears open in this regard.

Perfume development with artificial intelligence

In 2018, Symrise announced that it had developed a method together with IBM Research (project name: Philyra) to create perfumes based on digital fragrance models with the help of artificial intelligence. The Group's press release states: *"Perfumery as an art has a long tradition and we have been using this wealth of experience for several hundred years. At the end of the 19th century, synthetic fragrances revolutionised our industry. With artificial intelligence, we are now crossing the next threshold. I am proud to be part of it, says New York perfumer David Apel."*

The photos on this page are taken from the Symrise image database and show impressions of research and development in the company.

2003 – 2024

Symrise in Holzminden, below: Weser plant, above Solling plant

Photos (above and top of next page) from the company's image database show Symrise employees from different countries and divisions.

2023 – Current situation at Symrise

Compared to the past, Symrise has developed very dynamically in the 2020s. Therefore, the following list can only provide a snapshot:

The company offers a total of around 30,000 products, for which it sources around 10,000 raw materials from more than 100 countries. It has more than 6,000 customers in over 150 countries, primarily in the perfume, cosmetics, food and beverage industries, as well as in the pharmaceutical industry. These also include manufacturers of food supplements and pet food. The company has a 10 per cent share of the global market for fragrances and flavours. This puts it in fourth place, just behind Givaudan.

Headquarters are still located in Holzminden and it is also the largest location of Symrise AG. The employees there work in research, development, production, marketing and sales, as well as in the corporate centre.

The company maintains regional headquarters in the United States (Teterboro, New Jersey), Brazil (São Paulo), Singapore and France (Rennes). Important production plants are located in Germany, France, Brazil, Mexico, Singapore, China and the United States. Symrise has further sales offices in over 40 countries.

The Merger to Symrise

Symrise is committed to sustainability and research.

Symrise employees

As of 31 December 2020, Symrise employed 12,435 people worldwide, in addition to 221 apprentices and trainees. The largest group (about 6,000) works in production and technology, 2,600 employees work in sales and marketing, and almost 2,000 employees work in research and development. Approximately 3,000 employees are employed at sites in Germany, and around 6,000 in the entire EMEA region (Europe-Middle East-Africa). Around 2,000 of the group's employees work in Latin America, with a further 2,000 in the Asia/Pacific region and 2,400 in North America. Broken down by division, 3,500 employees work in the Scent & Care segment, while more than 7,000 employees work in the Taste, Nutrition & Health segment. 1,626 employees work in Group-wide functions.

Sustainability efforts

At Symrise, one of the company's main objectives is: "*We develop sustainable, safe and tailor-made products that ensure quality of life, beauty and well-being. We are aware of our responsibility for a future-oriented world.*" With regard to transparent sustainability reporting, Symrise states that, as an active member of Global Compact, the company is guided by both their universal principles for responsible corporate governance and the United Nations' Sustainable Development Goals (SDGs). All information is subject to external review and documented: "*With our sustainability reporting, we meet the guidelines of the Global Reporting Initiative (GRI) in the version of the GRI Standards (2021), including all updates from previous years.*"

In 2023, Symrise joined the following new initiatives, commitments and partnerships, and/or signed the corresponding declarations: Renewable Carbon Initiative, Low Carbon Transition Project and ProSpecieRara.

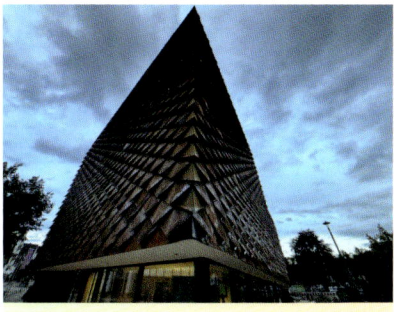

Sensoria - the house of fragrances and flavours

In October 2024 and 150 years after the founding of Wilhelm Haarmann's vanillin factory, Sensoria - House of Fragrances and Flavours will open in Holzminden. Located directly on the Weser bridge, the architecturally sophisticated building welcomes visitors to the town. Sensoria presents the fascinating world of fragrances and flavours in themed areas. Visitors are invited to wander through time and space and can learn more about the historical and scientific background. Sensoria highlights the often surprising importance of the senses in everyday life.

In its annual corporate report, Symrise also documents the company's sustainability strategy, which has won several awards in recent years.

Summary and outlook

Over the course of its history, the Holzminden-based company has evolved from a manufacturer of chemical or nature-identical fragrances and flavourings into a producer of complex - preferably natural - additives in the areas of nutrition and health.

This development is in line with the ambitions of Wilhelm Haarmann, who laid the foundations for the company in 1874. Haarmann was always on the lookout for innovations, new products and new markets. The battles for patent rights fought together with Ferdinand Tiemann in the 19th century showed how important research and development had always been to the Holzminden-based company.

Vanillin was first artificially reproduced by Wilhelm Haarmann 150 years ago and is now the world's most important flavouring agent, with an estimated production volume of 15,000 tonnes per year. Vanillin is still produced from the raw materials eugenol and guaiacol. However, a microbiological process has been developed for eugenol. This vanillin, like the vanillin produced from ferulic acid, is considered a natural flavouring. Guaiacol and, above all, lignin, which is found in wood and is mainly a byproduct of paper production, are the base materials for synthetic vanillin production.

Today, Symrise is committed to the sustainable cultivation of natural vanilla in Madagascar and the production of natural vanilla flavouring. Contrary to the claims of Wilhelm Haarmann and Ferdinand Tiemann, it has now been recognised that the natural vanilla flavour is not based solely on the vanillin contained in vanilla (around two percent), but is created by the interaction of a number of other substances. It has to be acknowledged that Haarmann and Tiemann's analytical techniques in the 19th century were nowhere near capable of discovering this wealth of flavour substances.

After 150 years of technical progress, we have realised that, on the one hand, we have to learn from nature and, on the other hand, we have to work in harmony with nature. The ambitious sustainability goals and the reverse integration of agricultural production processes are factors with which Symrise wants to meet the challenges of the present and the future. Today, Symrise would no longer grow lavender on the Burgberg. Instead, it is involved in the cultivation of aromatic plants in France; organic bananas for baby food in Ecuador; acerola cherries from north-east Brazil; natural vanilla from Madagascar, from which Symrise brought the first Fairtrade acerola powder onto the market; and onions for the company are now grown on a large scale in the fields in the Weserbergland.

Onion field in the Weserbergland

The Merger to Symrise

In contrast to the past, the Holzminden-based company now concentrates on the flavour of natural vanilla and is involved in the cultivation and processing of vanilla in Madagascar.

Appendix

Literature and sources

Literature used and recommendations

Becker, Dörte: „Vanillin – seit 150 Jahren ein Aroma der Zukunft der Lebensmittelindustrie", Rheinisch-westfälische Zeitschrift für Volkskunde, 53. Jg., Bonn und Münster 2008, S. 235-260

Coordination gegen BAYER-Gefahren (Hrsg.): IG Farben – Von Anilin bis Zwangsarbeit – Zur Geschichte von BASF, BAYER, Hoechst und anderen deutschen Chemie-Konzernen, Stuttgart, 1995

Gennermann, Paulina S.: Eine Geschichte mit Geschmack – Die Natur synthetischer Aromastoffe im 20. Jahrhundert am Beispiel Vanillin, Oldenburg 2023

Gerberding, Carl-Heinz: Erfüllte Jahre – Private Aufzeichnungen aus 65 Jahren, 1922 – 1987, Holzminden, 1991

Grimm, Hans-Ulrich: Die Suppe lügt – Die schöne neue Welt des Essens, München, 2014

Haarmann und Reimer GmbH: Das H&R Buch Parfum – Aspektes des Duftes, Geschichte, Herkunft, Entwicklung. Lexikon der Duftbausteine., Hamburg, 1991

Haarmann & Reimer GmbH (Hrsg.): Geruch und Geschmack – Ein Einblick in Tätigkeiten und Aufgaben eines Unternehmens der Riechstoff- und Geschmackstoffindustrie, Holzminden, 1974

Haarmann und Reimer GmbH: H-&-R-Duftatlas – Damen-Noten, Herren-Noten – Duftlandschaft des internationalen Marktes, Hamburg, 2. Aufl. 1991

Haarmann und Reimer GmbH: H-&-R-Duftatlas – Herren-Noten – Duftlandschaft des internationalen Marktes, Hamburg, 1985

Klammt, Karlheinz: „DRAGOCO – ein globales Familienunternehmen in Altendorf", Altendorf – Erinnerungen und Geschichten, Holzminden, 2008, S. 277-283

Koch, Hans-Werner: „Haarmann & Reimer", Altendorf – Erinnerungen und Geschichten, Holzminden, 2008, S. 271-277

Kretschmer, Paul: Die Weser-Solling-Stadt Holzminden – wie sie wurde, was sie ist, Holzminden, 1981

Krueger, Thomas: Arbeit, Holz und Porzellan – Carl I. und die Wirtschaftspolitik im 18. Jahrhundert – Der Weserdistrict –, Holzminden, 2013

Kuhse, Björn: Wilhelm Haarmann auf den Spuren der Vanille / Forscher, Unternehmer und Pionier der Riechstoffe, Holzminden, 2012

Müller-Grünow, Robert: Die Geheime Macht der Düfte – Warum wir unserem Geruchssinn mehr vertrauen sollten, Hamburg, 2018

Piech, Roland: Wiege einer Industrie – Düfte und Aromen aus Mitteldeutschland, Leipzig, 2022

Preußen, Wilhelm Karl Prinz von: „65 Jahre DRAGOCO", Jahrbuch für den Landkreis Holzminden 1984, Bd 2, S. 98-103.

Schwedt, Georg: Am Anfang war das Vanillin: Die Väter der Aromen-Industrie in Holzminden, Norderstedt, 2017

Seeliger, Matthias (Hrsg.): Holzminden im Aufbau – Luftaufnahmen aus dem Jahr 1956, Holzminden, 2005

Stanzl, Klaus: „Die Industrie der Riechstoffe im 19. Jahrhundert", Mitteilungen der Fachgruppe Geschichte der Chemie 26, 2020, S. 142—167

Vaupel, Elisabeth: (Hrsg.): Ersatzstoffe im Zeitalter der Weltkriege – Geschichte, Bedeutung, Perspektiven, München 2021

Vaupel, Elisabeth: Ersatzgewürze (1916–1948) – Der Chemie-Nobelpreisträger Hermann Staudinger und der Kunstpfeffer, Technikgeschichte Bd. 78 (2011) 2, S. 91-122

Vaupel, Elisabeth: „Ersatz für die Naturvanille –Rezeption und rechtliche Behandlung der Aromastoffe Vanillin und Ethylvanillin in Deutschland (1874–2011). In: Ferrum 89 (2017), S. 44–55.

Vogelmann, Margot: „Wilhelm Haarmann und seine Zeit", Jahrbuch für den Landkreis Holzminden 1986, Bd 4, S. 58-99.

Manuscripts

Collin, Gerhard: Die Geschichte der Dragoco, maschinenschriftlich, Holzminden o.J.

Grohs, Wolfram: Auf den Spuren der Familien Haarmann in der weiteren Region Holzminden – ein Beitrag zur Stadtgeschichte in lexikalischer Form, Holzminden 2014

Archives, collections and other sources

Firmen-Archiv Symrise
Archiv des Betriebsrates von Symrise
Stadtarchiv Holzminden | Regionalarchiv
Bundesarchiv - Akten Vanillin-Konvention
Sammlung Gerberding
Transcript of the ‚Haus-Chronik' der Familie Wilhelm Haarmann, Höxter

Annual reports and company publications:
  Haarmann & Reimer
  Dragoco
  Symrise
  Th. Geyer
Various issues of the company magazines:
  Berichte von Schimmel & Co
  Dragoco Berichte
  dragoco report,
  H&R Contact,
  Team Spirit, Symrise

Internet sources:

For the research for this book, publicly accessible online encyclopaedias and information platforms were also consulted, whose comprehensive content provided a valuable basis for a fundamental orientation in the field of chemical and economic history.

https://zeitpunkt.nrw/ – Zeitungsportal NRW
Das vom Land NRW geförderte Projekt digitalisiert Lokalzeitungen aus NRW im Zeitraum von 1801-1945.

Picture credits:

Bundesarchiv: 59 (2), 70,
Firmenarchiv Symrise: 11, 14, 15 (3), 20 (3), 23, 24, 25, 30, 32 (8), 33 (4), 34 u., 35, 36 (2), 37 re. (3), 38, 39 u., 40 (2), 41 o., 42 (3), 43 (3), 44 o., 45 (2), 46 (2), 47 (2), 48, 49 (2), 53 (2), 56 (2), 57 (3), 60 (2), 62 o., u., 63 re., 64, 65 o., 67, 68 (2), 69 u., 77, 78, 80, 81, 84, 87, 88, 90, 93 o., 94 (3), 96 (2), 97 o., 98 (2), 99 (5), 100 (3), 101 (5), 100 o., 107 u. (2), 109 (3), 110 (4), 111 (2), 112 (3), 113 (3), 114 u. (3), 116 o., 117 (4), 118 (2), 119 (2), 120, 121 (2), 122 (2), 124 (2), 127 o., 128 u., 130 (2), 131, 132 o., 133, 145, 159 (2)
Bilddatenbank Symrise: 141 (2), 142, 144, 151 (4), 152 (2), 153 o. (2), 155
Historische Unterlagen Betriebsrat Symrise: 16, 17, 21 (2), 22, 54, 55, 63 o., 69 (2), 71, 72 (2), 73, 74, 75, 76 u., 85 (2), 86 (2), 91, 92,
Nds. Staatsarchiv Wolfenbüttel: 18 o. (STAWO K 14739)
Stadtarchiv Holzminden: 10 (2), 12 o., 18 u., 27, 42 li., 52, 58 (3), 61, 65 (3), 66 (4), 76 o., 79, 89 (2), 95 (4), 97 (2), 98 o., 100 (2), 106 (2), 107 (2), 114 o. (2), 115 (2), 116 u., 126 (2)
Stadtarchiv Höxter: 34
Sammlung Gerberding: 96 o., 108 (2), 112 u., 115 u., 128 o., 129 (2), 132 u.,
Sammlung Stefan Nowak: 103 (3)
Jörg Mitzkat: 12 u.,147 (3), 153 re. (2), 154 u.,
Sammlung Verlag Jörg Mitzkat: 19, 26, 41 u., 44 u., 62 mi., 93 u., 123 (2), 125 (2), 127 u., 137, 146, 148, 150, 154 o.,
Täglicher Anzeiger Holzminden: 143, 149
Wikipedia: 13, 20 o., 31, 49 re.,
zeitpunkt nrw: 23 re., 31, 37 u., 39 o.,

Thank you for your support, important tips and further information:

Elisabeth Belik
Wolfgang Bellmer
Dr. Heinz-Jürgen Bertram
Cristof Bode
Harald Feist
Horst-Otto Gerberding
Dr. Wolfram Grohs
Karl-Heinz Huchthausen
Karlheinz Klammt
Bernhard Kott
Julian Kühn
Stefan Nowak
Dominik Rzepka
Dr. Christoph Sandforth
Dr. Wolfgang Schäfer
Caroline Schütte
Dr. Matthias Seeliger
Dr. Sven Siegel

View over the premises of Haarmann & Reimer across Holzminden towards Köterberg, 1960s

View from the main building of Dragoco over Holzminden in the direction of Köterberg, 1950s

Dragoco Werbung, 1970er
Dragoco advertising, 1970s

Haarmann & Reimer Werbung, 1970er
Haarmann & Reimer advertising, 1970s

Dragoco Kantine mit *Tante Mieze*, 1950er
Dragoco canteen with *Aunt Mieze*, 1950s